Amazing Science Devotions for Children's Ministry

D1054055

Group

Loveland, Colorado

AMAZING SCIENCE DEVOTIONS FOR CHILDREN'S MINISTRY
Copyright © 1999 Group Publishing, Inc.

Visit our website: **group.com**

CREDITS
Contributing Authors: Sheila Halasz, Valery L. Lytle, Debbie Trafton O'Neal, Ruth Reaxin, Julie Pyle Samuels, and Larry Shallenberger
Book Acquisitions Editor: Lori Haynes Niles
Editor: Julie Meiklejohn
Creative Development Editor: Dave Thornton
Chief Creative Officer: Joani Schultz
Copy Editor: Debbie Gowensmith
Art Director: Jean Bruns
Cover Art Director: Jeff A. Storm
Computer Graphic Artist: Joyce Douglas
Illustrators: Mike Wright and Jan Knudson
Production Manager: Peggy Naylor

Library of Congress Cataloging-in-Publication Data
Amazing science devotions for children's ministry / [contributing authors, Sheila Halasz ... et al.].
      p. cm.
  Includes indexes
  ISBN 978-0-7644-2105-1
  1. Christian education of children. 2. Science--Problems, exercises, etc. 3. Christian education--Activity programs.
  I. Halasz, Sheila. II. Group Publishing.
  BV1536.5.A53 1998   98-21717
  268'.432--dc21   CIP

16 15 14 13   13 12 11 10
Printed in the United States of America.

Amazing Science Devotions for Children's Ministry • Rock • Light • Salt • Living Wa

ontents

DEVOTIONS

Use water to simulate the lens of an eye to help kids explore how they can use the light of Christ to "see" God's plan more clearly.

Show kids that just as the pupils of their eyes dilate or contract automatically, kids can choose to automatically trust God even in scary situations.

As kids experience different sound waves, they learn about different ways of "hearing" God's Word.

Use dactylography (the study of fingerprints) to help kids discover that God always knows "whodunit."

Kids experience feeling dizzy and off-balance as they explore God's "solid as a rock" love.

Kids explore the amazing way spiders catch their food as they learn more about God's wonderful creations.

Kids explore a solar eclipse as they learn that God is always there, even when he feels far away.

Kids experience miniature "earthquakes" as they explore how to build their lives on Jesus.

wer ● Heavens ● Earth ● Wind ● Bread ● Storm ● Garden ● Compass ● Rainbow ● Creation

Power * Heavens * Earth * Wind * Bread * Storm * Garden * Compass * Rainbow * Creati

Power * Heavens * Earth * Wind * Bread * Storm * Garden * Compass * Rainbow * Creati

Introduction

"How is a rainbow formed?" "Why are my fingerprints different from anyone else's?" "What makes popcorn pop?"

Kids are fascinated by the way the world works, and they love to learn about the science behind everyday phenomena. Kids especially enjoy experimenting with objects and scientific properties as they discover firsthand how these things work. This natural fascination is a wonderful jumping-off place to help kids learn about God's power and his plan for each of his children.

You may have wondered how to tap into this natural fascination. *Amazing Science Devotions for Children's Ministry* is your answer!

Each of these ten- to fifteen-minute devotions gives kids a "wow!" experience as they learn more about the incredible world God created. Many of the devotions allow kids to get involved in the action right along with the teacher. Then, through solid discussion, kids discover more about the powerful God who created the whole universe and cares greatly for each of them.

The devotions in *Amazing Science Devotions for Children's Ministry* make great children's sermons, fun Sunday school lesson introductions, or excellent activities any time you want to give kids' faith a little boost while indulging their natural curiosity about how and why things work.

Kids will experience many different areas of scientific exploration in *Amazing Science Devotions for Children's Ministry,* including biology and the natural world; physics; earth science properties of gravity, magnetism, and light; and lots more.

Each devotion includes clear instructions and explanations, and you'll need only a few easy-to-obtain supplies for each one. You'll find helpful hints and fun extension ideas in the "Scientist's Strategy" boxes.

Now it's time for you and your kids to don your lab coats, pull out your magnifying glasses, and prepare to have tons of science fun while learning about God and his wonderful creation.

Happy experimenting!

Rock • Light • Salt • Living Water • Amazing Science Devotions for Children's Ministry

Seeing Is Believing

EXPLORATION ELEMENT: Use water to simulate the lens of an eye to help kids explore how they can use the light of Christ to "see" God's plan more clearly.

BIBLE BENCHMARK: "Now we see but a poor reflection as in a mirror; then we shall see face to face. Now I know in part; then I shall know fully, even as I am fully known" (1 Corinthians 13:12).

SUPPLIES: You'll need a Bible, coated twenty-gauge wire (from a hardware store), sharp scissors or wire cutters, pencils or pens, water, several bowls to hold the water, and newspapers or magazines.

OPTIONAL SUPPLIES: You may want two magnifying glasses; an assortment of small items including feathers, leaves, and small rocks; and an ink pad and paper.

PREPARATION: Cut a six- to seven-inch piece of wire for each child. On a table, set out bowls of water and newspapers or magazines. Close all the shutters, blinds, or drapes ahead of time so the room will be dark when the lights are off.

sk:

• **What do you need in order to see the world around you?**

Say: **We need our eyes and light to see the world. Let's do an experiment that will show us how our eyes help us to see God's world.**

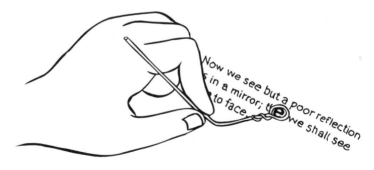

Give each child a piece of wire and a pencil, and say: **I'd like you to twist one end of your piece of wire around the pencil to make a small, round loop.** Demonstrate this, and then help the kids do it. Say: **Now bend your piece of wire so you have a nice sharp corner between your loop and the straight part of the wire. The straight part will be your handle.** Demonstrate this, and then help the kids do it.

Have kids dip their wire loops carefully into the bowls of water and then lift out the loops slowly so a drop of water stays in each loop. Have kids hold their wire loops over the newspapers or magazines and look through the "lenses" at the letters. Ask:

● **How do the letters look when you see them through the water?**

Say: **If the drop of water in your loop curves outward, it is a convex lens. This is just like the lenses we have in our eyes, and it makes the letters look bigger. If the drop of water in your loop curves inward, it is a concave lens. It makes the letters look smaller.**

Give kids a few minutes to look at different kinds of type in the magazines and newspapers, and then ask:

● **Would we be able to see these things if there wasn't any light? Explain.**

Say: **Let's see what happens when we turn out the lights.** Have a child turn out all the lights in the room, and ask:

● **Now how well can you see the magazines and newspapers?**

● **Do your lenses work without light?**

Say: **Our lenses and the light work together to help us see. We need them both.**

Turn the lights back on, and read 1 Corinthians 13:12 aloud. Say: **This verse tells us we can't see God's truth very well by ourselves; we need help.** Ask:

● **Who do you think can help us see God's truth more clearly?**

Scientist's Strategy

Warn the kids before you turn out the lights in case some kids are afraid of the dark. Have kids sit next to you if necessary.

Scientist's Strategy

As an additional activity, have kids use magnifying glasses to look at a human hair, a feather, a leaf, a small rock, and each other's fingerprints.

Say: **God gave us Jesus to help us understand God better. Just as we can see things with our eyes better if we have light, we can best see the way God wants us to live when the light of Jesus helps us see our path.** Ask:

● **How does Jesus provide the light we need to help us find the right way whenever we need it?**

Say: **Letting Jesus into your life is like turning on the lights or lighting a fire. Jesus lights up your whole life. And you can see God more clearly with the light Jesus gives you. The better you get to know Jesus, the more you'll understand God.**

Look!

EXPLORATION ELEMENT: Show kids that just as the pupils of their eyes dilate or contract automatically, kids can choose to automatically trust God even in scary situations.

BIBLE BENCHMARK: "The Lord is my light and my salvation—whom shall I fear? The Lord is the stronghold of my life—of whom shall I be afraid?" (Psalm 27:1).

SUPPLIES: You'll need a Bible, several flashlights, and a large mirror several kids can look into at the same time (or enough hand mirrors for each child to have one).

OPTIONAL SUPPLIES: You may want a small lamp or a candle and matches.

PREPARATION: None is needed.

Scientist's Strategy

If your room gets completely dark when the lights are turned out, have a small lamp or candle available so kids will be able to see each other's eyes when the room lights are turned out.

Open your Bible to the book of Psalms, and read Psalm 27:1 to the group. Say: **We all have**

Power * Heavens * Earth * Wind * Bread * Storm * Garden * Compass * Rainbow * Creati

times in our lives when we are afraid or lonely. But God's Word reminds us that God is always with us! God will guide us through our lives, and we have nothing to fear.

Have kids form pairs. Say: **I'd like for you to look into each other's eyes, especially looking at the black circle, or the pupil, in the middle. When we're in normal light, the pupils of our eyes are a certain size to let in just the right amount of light so we can see clearly. If we're in bright light, our pupils contract, or get smaller, to keep the light from hurting our eyes. If we turn off the light, our pupils dilate, or get bigger, to let in more light so we can see better.**

Turn off the light, and have kids look at their partners' eyes again. Ask:

● **Do your partner's eyes look the same? What is happening to his or her pupils?**

● **Can you still see as clearly as you could with the lights on?**

Give each child (or group of children) a small flashlight, and have children stand in front of a mirror (or give each child a hand mirror). Say: **Quickly turn on your flashlight and shine it across your face while you look into the mirror. Can you see your pupils change in response to the light? We can't choose to make our eyes do this; it happens whether we want it to or not. This is called an involuntary action or response; it happens automatically.**

In the same way, we can choose to automatically trust God.

Whenever we're feeling lonely or afraid, we can remember that God is always with us. This experiment can remind us that although we can't always choose the situations we're in or the way we feel, we can automatically trust God no matter what. We can stop and remind ourselves that we have nothing to fear when God is with us.

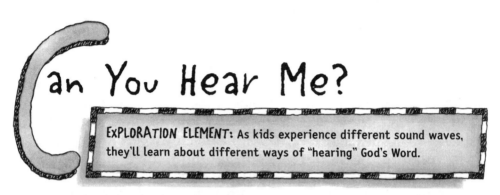

Can You Hear Me?

EXPLORATION ELEMENT: As kids experience different sound waves, they'll learn about different ways of "hearing" God's Word.

BIBLE BENCHMARK: "He replied, 'Blessed rather are those who hear the word of God and obey it' " (Luke 11:28).

SUPPLIES: You'll need a Bible; a metal spoon and a three-foot length of string for each student; and various objects such as an apple, a pencil, and a cardboard tube.

PREPARATION: None is needed.

Read Luke 11:28 to the group. Ask:
- **Where can we find the Word of God?**
- **Do you think it's easy or difficult to hear God's Word? Why?**
- **What are some ways you hear God's Word?**
- **Do you ever hear God's Word from your parents? from friends?**

Say: **Sometimes it's easy to hear the Word of God. And we can hear God's Word in many different ways. One way we hear God's Word is by using our ears. This experiment will help us to better understand one way we can hear the words God has for us.**

*Power * Heavens * Earth * Wind * Bread * Storm * Garden * Compass * Rainbow * Creati*

Have kids form pairs, and give each child a metal spoon and a three-foot length of string. Have one partner tie a spoon in the center of a length of string and then put the ends of the string in his or her ears. Then say: **Now have your partner gently hit your spoon with his or her spoon.** Give kids enough time for each partner to have a chance to do this. Ask:

● **What happened when you hit the spoon gently?**

● **What do you think would happen if you hit the spoon harder?**

● **How does the sound change from the time the spoon is first hit until you can't hear it anymore?**

● **Why do you think this happens when the vibration of the spoon slows down?**

● **Do you think the sound would be different if you hit the spoon on the string with another object?**

Say: **Let's try it!** Show kids the other objects, and give them a few minutes to try hitting the spoon with the objects. Ask:

● **What differences did you hear between the objects?**

Say: **The scientific explanation for what happens is this: Sound travels through solids, like the spoon and the string, better than it travels through the air. Sound travels by vibrating, or moving back and forth very quickly. These vibrations are called sound waves.**

One way to hear God's Word is by using our ears. Just as the vibration of the spoon sometimes sounded different, a familiar part of God's Word sometimes has a whole new meaning for us. Or instead of hearing God's Word with our ears, we might read

it in the Bible or hear it from our parents, our pastor, or a friend and understand it in a new way. Isn't it great to know that God has so many ways for us to hear his Word? Ask:

● Can you think of any new ways you might try to hear God's Word this week?

Whodunit?

EXPLORATION ELEMENT: Use dactylography (the study of fingerprints) to help kids discover that God always knows "whodunit."

BIBLE BENCHMARK: "You know my folly, O God; my guilt is not hidden from you" (Psalm 69:5).

SUPPLIES: You'll need a Bible; a dark-colored plate made of pottery, plastic, or glass; a cookie; talcum; a small, soft paintbrush; pencils; index cards; a "Fingerprint Chart" (p. 16) for each child; transparent tape; and baby wipes.

OPTIONAL SUPPLIES: You may want a bag of cookies.

PREPARATION: Set out a clean plate with one half-eaten cookie and many crumbs on it. Make sure you are the only person to handle the plate, and be sure to make a few clear fingerprints on the plate.

Say: **Someone has eaten the cookies I wanted to share with you.** Ask:

● **Does anyone know how to figure out who did this?**

Say: **I know of an experiment we can do that will help us find out who did this. We're going to be detectives.** Have one child pour a little bit of talcum on the plate. Have a second child use the paintbrush to brush the talcum over the plate. Ask:

● **What do you see?**

Say: **Everybody's fingers have a little bit of oil on them.**

Power ● Heavens ● Earth ● Wind ● Bread ● Storm ● Garden ● Compass ● Rainbow ● Creatio

When we touch something, we always leave a little bit of oil on whatever we touch. Ask:

● **How do you think these fingerprints got their shapes?**

Say: **The fingerprints we leave behind are called latent fingerprints. Let's see if we can make pictures of our fingerprints.** Give each child two index cards, a pencil, and ten one-inch pieces of transparent tape. Say: **First I'd like you to rub your pencil on one of your index cards to make a smudge. After you've done that, rub the fingertip of your right-hand index finger over the smudge until your fingertip is silver-colored.** Give kids a few moments to do this, and then say: **Now I'd like you to stick one piece of tape onto your fingertip and press down. Then take the piece of tape off your finger and stick it on your other index card. Be sure to label your fingerprints. Label the fingerprint you just took "index finger, right hand." Continue this way until you have a print of each finger.** While kids are working, make your own fingerprints. After kids have finished, give them baby wipes to wash their hands. Ask:

● **What do you notice about your fingerprints?**

Say: **The science of identifying fingerprints is called dactylography** (dak-tuh-LAH-gruh-fy). Distribute the "Fingerprint Chart" (p. 16), and say: **Fingerprints have three different shapes: loops, whorls, and arches.** Ask:

● **Which shape are your fingerprints?**

After children identify the shapes of their fingerprints, have them form pairs or trios and compare fingerprints. Ask:

● **Are any of your fingerprints exactly alike?**

Say: **It's time for you to act like detectives. No two sets of fingerprints are exactly the same. God made them all different. Let's compare them to the fingerprints on the plate. Let's see if anybody's fingerprints match the fingerprints on the plate.** Have the children compare all of their fingerprints to the fingerprints on the plate. Let them discover that the fingerprints are yours. Ask:

● **Was anybody looking when I took the cookies?**

● **Have you ever done something wrong when nobody was looking?**

● **Were you afraid of being caught? Explain.**

Read aloud Psalm 69:5, and say: **God sees everything. He knows what we do even when we think nobody's looking. God is everywhere and sees everything, so he doesn't need to use fingerprints. God sees us when we think about doing bad things, and he wants to help us make the right choices. We need to remember that we can't hide our actions from God.**

FINGERPRINT CHART

LOOP PATTERN   **WHORL PATTERN**   **ARCH PATTERN**

Permission to photocopy this chart from *Amazing Science Devotions for Children's Ministry* granted for local church use. Copyright © Group Publishing, Inc., P.O. Box 481, Loveland, CO 80539.

Spinning in God's Grace

EXPLORATION ELEMENT: Kids experience feeling dizzy and off-balance as they explore God's "solid as a rock" love.

BIBLE BENCHMARK: "The Lord is my rock, my fortress and my deliverer; my God is my rock, in whom I take refuge" (Psalm 18:2a).

SUPPLIES: You'll need a Bible.

PREPARATION: Take kids to an open area for this devotion.

Power * Heavens * Earth * Wind * Bread * Storm * Garden * Compass * Rainbow * Creatio

Have kids form pairs (be sure partners are similar in size). Say: **One person in each pair needs to stand very still. The other partner in each pair will need to put his or her arms straight out to the sides, spin around five times as fast as possible, and then quickly hold on to his or her partner's shoulders. Ready? Go!** After kids have tried this, let them switch roles and do it again. Then ask:

- **How did you feel after you spun around?**
- **Why do you think you got dizzy?**
- **What did it feel like to have someone to hold on to?**

Say: **You have liquid in your inner ear that helps your body know if you are balanced or not. When you spin around so quickly, the liquid in your ear begins to move as well in order to keep you balanced. When your body suddenly stops spinning around, the liquid continues to move slightly. This movement is what makes you feel dizzy. When you feel dizzy, sometimes you need something or someone to hold on to so you won't fall down.**

Just as spinning around made you dizzy, sometimes things in your life can spin you around and make you feel off-balance and dizzy. Ask:

- **What are some things that can happen in your life to make you feel dizzy?**
- **Who can you hold on to when your life makes you dizzy?**

Say: **God is someone solid you can hold on to when things in your life throw you off-balance. God will lead you on the straight path and keep you balanced. When the world makes you dizzy, it's very important to meet with God and ask him to balance your life with his guidance.**

Read aloud Psalm 18:2a. Ask:

- **Has God ever been a rock, a fortress, or a deliverer in your life? How?**

If it is possible, arrange for someone to share a testimony of how God has worked in his or her life.

Say: **The next time your life makes you feel dizzy, remember that you can lean on God, and he'll help you keep your balance.**

ock • Light ...zing Science Devotions for Children's Ministry

Spiders, God's Creations

> **EXPLORATION ELEMENT:** Kids will explore the amazing way spiders catch their food as they learn more about God's wonderful creatures.

BIBLE BENCHMARK: "And God said, 'Let the land produce living creatures according to their kinds: livestock, creatures that move along the ground, and wild animals, each according to its kind.' And it was so. God made the wild animals according to their kinds, the livestock according to their kinds, and all the creatures that move along the ground according to their kinds. And God saw that it was good" (Genesis 1:24-25).

SUPPLIES: You'll need a Bible, thread, and scissors.

OPTIONAL SUPPLIES: You may want black construction paper and white crayons or glue.

PREPARATION: Cut four one-yard pieces of thread. Form a large X by tying the pieces together (see the diagram below). Set the X on the floor.

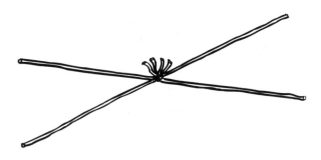

Ask:
- **How many of you have ever seen a spider?**
- **Why do you think some people are afraid of spiders?**

Say: **Spiders are an amazing part of God's creation. We're going to learn a bit more about spiders today.** Ask:
- **What can you tell me about spiders?**

● **Where do spiders live?**

Say: **Spiders spend much of their lives spinning webs to catch food. If you ever take a walk in the morning when there's still dew on the grass, you can see some spectacular spider webs. Today we're going to discover just how amazing a spider is by experiencing the same sensation a spider feels when something lands on its web.**

If you have time, let kids design their own spider webs on black construction paper using white crayons or glue.

I need four volunteers to hold the four ends of thread. I also need the volunteers to close their eyes. No peeking, please. I am going to be a tiny insect and land on your web. See if you can tell when I am landing on the web. If you feel me land on the web, raise your hand.

"Land" on one part of the web by tapping it with one finger. After kids raise their hands to indicate they felt it, say: **If you think I landed on your side of the web, keep your hand raised.**

Have kids take turns holding the ends of the web until they tire of the game. Then ask:

● **Was it easy to feel the insect when it landed on the spider web?**

● **Why do you think spiders build webs?**

Read aloud Genesis 1:24-25, and then say: **God created many amazing and wonderful things in our world. Spiders are beautiful creatures designed by God. He did not create them to scare us. Spiders won't hurt us if we don't bother them because they're very afraid of humans. Also, there are very few spiders that are poisonous to humans. The next time you see a spider, take the time to watch it and see where it's going and what it's doing. If you're lucky, you just might get the opportunity to watch it weave a web. As you're watching, remember to thank God for all the amazing creatures he created.**

ower * Heavens * Storm * Garden * Compass * Rainbow * Creation

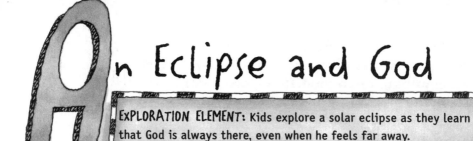

An Eclipse and God

EXPLORATION ELEMENT: Kids explore a solar eclipse as they learn that God is always there, even when he feels far away.

BIBLE BENCHMARKS: "God made two great lights—the greater light to govern the day and the lesser light to govern the night. He also made the stars. God set them into the expanse of the sky to give light on the earth, to govern the day and the night, and to separate light from darkness. And God saw that it was good" (Genesis 1:16-18).

"Never will I leave you; never will I forsake you" (Hebrews 13:5b).

SUPPLIES: You'll need a Bible, a flashlight, a tennis ball, and a basketball.

PREPARATION: It would be a good idea to practice this experiment ahead of time so you can correctly space the flashlight and the balls.

sk:

• **Can anyone tell me what a solar eclipse is?**

Say: **Let me show you how an eclipse happens.**

Ask two kids to be your helpers. Give one child the flashlight (representing the sun), and give the other child the basketball (representing the earth). You will be controlling the tennis ball (representing the moon).

Have the child holding the "sun" shine it directly onto the "earth." Rotate the "moon" around the earth. Be sure to rotate it in the sun's light. Say: **Notice that the moon sometimes blocks out the sunlight and makes the earth dark in the middle of the day! This is called an eclipse. If we didn't know what caused the eclipse, its effect would be frightening, wouldn't it? Now that we know, it is amazing!**

Let kids take turns holding the flashlight and the tennis ball to form an eclipse.

Read aloud Genesis 1:16-18, and say: **God made the sun, the moon, and the earth; set them into orbit; and said they were good. So God must have known that eclipses would happen sometimes. Sometimes you may feel that circumstances in your life are like eclipses. When everything seems to go wrong, you may feel like you're in the shadow. During an eclipse, the sky looks dark, but we know that the light is still there. When you have troubles in your life, you may not always be able to feel God there, but you can know that he is!** Ask:

● **Can you think of something that happened in your life that reminds you of an eclipse? What happened?**

Say: **Think of a terrible, awful day you've had. Everything seemed to be going wrong.** Ask:

● **How did you feel?**

Read aloud Hebrews 13:5b, and ask:

● **Why is this good news?**

● **What does this tell us about God?**

● **Does an eclipse tell us anything about God?**

● **How might knowing that God has a plan for everything that happens change the way you feel about a bad day?**

Say: **Think about our eclipse experiment. Pretend that your life is represented by the basketball.** Ask:

● **What in your life can you compare the flashlight to?**

● **What about the tennis ball?**

Say: **Troubles seem to put a shadow on your life. This is when God wants you to really trust him. God wants you to know that just as the sun is still shining during an eclipse, he is always there during your troubled times.**

Jiggle, Shake, Quake

> **EXPLORATION ELEMENT:** Kids experience miniature "earthquakes" as they explore how to build their lives on Jesus.

BIBLE BENCHMARK: "So then, just as you received Christ Jesus as Lord, continue to live in him, rooted and built up in him, strengthened in the faith as you were taught, and overflowing with thankfulness" (Colossians 2:6-7).

SUPPLIES: You'll need a Bible, two 9x12-inch aluminum baking pans, four boxes of flavored gelatin, two cups, marshmallows, and a box of toothpicks.

PREPARATION: Prepare two pans of flavored gelatin (use two boxes for each pan). Chill the pans of flavored gelatin overnight.

Ask:

● **Have you ever been in an earthquake or seen the results of one on TV?**

● **What causes earthquakes?**

Say: **Earthquakes are caused when the tectonic plates under the surface of the earth shift. Sometimes they run into each other, and this causes the ground above the plates to shift and shake. We're going to experience miniature earthquakes today.**

Have children form two groups, and have kids sit in their groups at a long table. Give each group a pan of flavored gelatin and a cup of marshmallows. Say: **The gelatin in your pan represents the earth,**

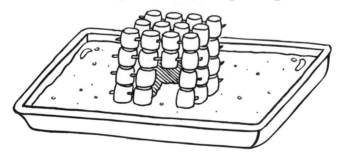

Power ● Heavens ● Earth ● Wind ● Bread ● Storm ● Garden ● Compass ● Rainbow ● Creatio

and the marshmallows are your building materials. Using the marshmallows, you'll need to build a house that can stand up by itself.** Give one group the box of toothpicks, and say: **I'm giving toothpicks to this group to use along with the marshmallows.**

After groups have built their houses, test them by shaking the table. Ask:

● **Which building didn't fall** (or didn't fall as easily)? **Why?**

Say: **Some places on earth sit on the place where tectonic plates come together. These places are called faults. In some fault areas, such as Southern California, it's important to build buildings with special reinforcements to keep the buildings from falling during earthquakes. The toothpicks one group used were kind of like the special reinforcements put into buildings in a fault area.** Ask:

● **What kinds of situations in your life might feel like an earthquake?**

Read aloud Colossians 2:6-7, and ask:

● **According to this Scripture, what do we need to do to reinforce our lives?**

● **What does this passage tell you about following Christ and doing what he says?**

● **How can you reinforce your life with Christ?**

Say: **Just as the toothpicks reinforced our marshmallow "buildings," God wants us to reinforce our lives with faith in his Son, Jesus. No matter what "earthquakes" or problems we may come across in our lives, God will strengthen us through our faith in Christ.**

Digging in the Dirt

EXPLORATION ELEMENT: Kids explore different materials found in ordinary dirt while discovering that learning more about God changes the way they view the world around them.

BIBLE BENCHMARK: "When I was a child, I talked like a child, I thought like a child, I reasoned like a child. When I became a man, I put childish ways behind me. Now we see but a poor reflection as in a mirror; then we shall see face to face. Now I know in part; then I shall know fully, even as I am fully known" (1 Corinthians 13:11-12).

SUPPLIES: You'll need a Bible, newspaper, a bucket of dirt, a dishpan, a strainer or a colander, several spoons, a magnifying glass, and a pitcher or watering can full of water.

OPTIONAL SUPPLIES: You may want a bucket of gravel or small pebbles.

PREPARATION: Spread newspaper over a table or on the floor. Place the dishpan and the bucket of dirt on the newspaper.

Read 1 Corinthians 13:11-12 to the group. Say: **This Bible passage tells us that as we grow older and learn more, we think about and talk about and do different things. Our faith in God is the same way. As we grow and learn more about God and his plan for our lives, we see things differently. Let's try an experiment to see how this idea works.**

Have kids gather around the bucket of dirt and the dishpan, and ask:

● **What do you see in this bucket?**

When kids answer "dirt," ask:

● **Are you sure that's all that's in here?**

Say: **Perhaps dirt is all you see right now.** Give one child the strainer, and have him or

Scientist's Strategy

For best results, make sure the dirt you scoop up before class has a variety of things in it. Ordinary garden dirt (not topsoil or potting soil) is best. For fun, try a bucket of gravel or small pebbles to sift and pour through the strainer to see if it produces similar results.

her hold it over the dishpan. Give several other children spoons, and have children scoop some of the dirt from the bucket into the strainer. Have kids take turns using the spoons to stir the dirt to sift the finer particles of dirt into the dishpan. As they do this, other things will begin to surface, such as bits of partially composted leaves, twigs, small pieces of gravel, and perhaps even a worm. Ask:

● **What is happening? What do you see as you sift and stir?**

Say: **Look with the magnifying glass at the debris left in the strainer.** Ask:

● **Is that what you would call "dirt"?**

Say: **Feel the dirt you've sifted out.** Ask:

● **How does it feel? Does it feel different from the dirt left in the bucket?**

Say: **Let's try adding water to wash the materials we found in the dirt. I wonder how that will change what we see.**

Pour the sifted dirt onto the newspaper, and carefully pour water into the strainer full of debris as the child continues to hold it over the dishpan. Ask:

● **What is happening now?**

● **Do you see anything that you didn't see before?**

● **How do you think this is like what happens in our lives when we learn more about God?**

Say: **Being a follower of God is exciting! We know that as we grow and learn about God and his world, we'll see things we never saw before.** Ask:

● **What things do you see differently now from the way you** saw them when you were younger?

• **What things don't you really understand about God now but hope to understand better as you grow older?**

• **What things might you not fully understand until you get to heaven?**

Say: **As our faith becomes stronger, things in our everyday lives will seem new and different, just like pouring water on the things we found in the dirt made them look different.**

Feel the Earth Move

ExPLORATION ELEMENT: Use the concept of soil erosion to help kids understand how we feel sometimes when it's hard to follow Jesus.

BIBLE BENCHMARK: "I have told you these things, so that in me you may have peace. In this world you will have trouble. But take heart! I have overcome the world" (John 16:33).

SUPPLIES: You'll need a Bible, newspaper, a large aquarium or a clear plastic storage box, potting soil or dirt, sand, a bucket, a small shovel or a large spoon, plant clippings, and a watering can or a pitcher full of water.

OPTIONAL SUPPLIES: You may want a dishpan or a large bowl.

PREPARATION: Spread newspaper over a table or on the floor. Place the aquarium, the potting soil, the sand, and the bucket on the newspaper.

Read aloud John 16:33 to the group. Say: **I have an experiment we can do to help us understand why Jesus said these words to his disciples.** Have kids gather around the items on the newspaper, and pour equal parts of soil and sand into the bucket. Give a student the small shovel, and ask him or her to mix the sand and soil together. Say:

I'm going to make a hill in the aquarium with this soil mixture. Pour the soil mixture into the aquarium, keeping the major portion of it at one end. Let kids help you build up this end to make a hill with a flat top.

Say: **Let's pretend this hill is the earth. Now it's going to rain!** Ask:

● **What do you think will happen to our hill when it rains?**

Gently pour water from the watering can to make it "rain" on the soil mixture. Ask:

● **What's happening to the hill?**

● **What do you think will happen if it rains harder? Why?**

Pour water a little faster from the watering can to make it rain harder.

Say: **The process of water moving the dirt is called erosion. Erosion happens when water or wind wear away the earth's surface over a period of time.** Ask:

● **Do you think there is any way to keep erosion from happening?**

If the hill has eroded too much or the dirt is too wet, re-form the hill by adding more dirt. If you need to, carefully drain excess water into a dishpan or bowl. Have several children help you insert the plant clippings into the hillside and on top of the hill. Say: **Let's try making it rain again.** Gently pour water from the watering can over the soil mixture. Ask:

● **Where does the soil go now that there are plants in the hillside?**

● **What else could we do to stop the erosion process?**

Let kids offer their suggestions about stopping the erosion process, and let them try some of their ideas if you have time. Ask:

● **How do you think erosion might be like the way we feel sometimes when it's difficult to follow Jesus?**

Say: **Jesus knew that sometimes it would be hard to be his disciples.** Ask:

● **Do you think Jesus knew that sometimes it would be hard for us to be his followers today, too? Why?**

● **What kinds of things might happen to cause us to question our faith and whether we believe Jesus' words or not?**

● **What can we do to help us stay close to Jesus?**

ck • Light • Salt • Living Water • Amazing Science Devotions for Children's Ministry

Say: **Jesus wants you to stay close to him; some things you can do to help you stay close to Jesus are praying, reading your Bible, or coming to church. Having Christian friends can also help us stay close to Jesus. When we stay close to Jesus and listen to God's Word, we can feel the peace Jesus offers us. This will keep us from experiencing "faith erosion."**

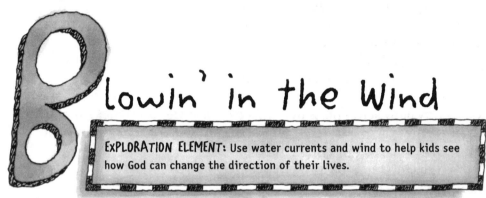

Blowin' in the Wind

EXPLORATION ELEMENT: Use water currents and wind to help kids see how God can change the direction of their lives.

BIBLE BENCHMARK: "The waters flooded the earth for a hundred and fifty days. But God remembered Noah and all the wild animals and the livestock that were with him in the ark, and he sent a wind over the earth, and the waters receded" (Genesis 7:24–8:1).

SUPPLIES: You'll need a Bible; newspaper; a large, clear glass bowl of water; a small toy boat that will float in the bowl; and talcum.

OPTIONAL SUPPLIES: You may need towels.

PREPARATION: Spread newspaper over a table or on the floor. Place the bowl of water on the newspaper.

Tell the story of Noah and the ark, or read the account found in Genesis before beginning this activity. Then read aloud Genesis 7:24–8:1 to the group.

Gather kids around the bowl of water. Say: **Let's pretend that the water in this bowl is the ocean. It looks pretty calm, doesn't it?** Put the toy boat in the bowl. Say: **The water still looks calm, but water always has some motion to it.** Have kids blow gently on the water surface. Ask:

● **What is happening to the water surface?**
● **Why does the wind make the water surface change?**
● **What happens to the boat when the water moves?**

Amazing Science Devotions for Children's Ministry • Rock • Light • Salt • Living Wa

Say: **Wind that blows across the surface of the water makes currents. A current is the movement of a liquid in a particular path or direction. Sometimes currents are really strong—currents in a river make the water travel around rocks and tree roots. A current in the ocean can be strong, too—strong enough to make the water change the path of other objects such as boats or people who are swimming.**

To help us see the currents in our ocean, let's add some talcum to the water surface.

Scientist's Strategy

Pairs of students will enjoy trying this activity on their own after you've demonstrated it to the class. Be sure to have towels available for any water spills!

Have one child sprinkle talcum on the surface of the water, and then have kids gently blow across the water surface again. Say: **The talcum helps us see how the water currents change the water's surface as the wind blows on the water.**

When God remembered Noah and the animals on the ark, he sent a wind over the earth so the waters would go down and there would be dry land again for the people and animals to live on. We can remember that the wind God sent cleared the way for people to live on the earth again.

In the Bible, the Holy Spirit sometimes acts in the form of the wind (Acts 2). Ask:

● **How do you think the wind might be kind of like God's Spirit in your life?**

● **What are ways God could change the direction of your life as the wind changed the direction of the water?**

Say: **If the way your life is going doesn't seem quite right,**

God's Spirit, like the wind, can help change the direction of your life. God will help you live the way he wants you to if you trust him and allow him to work in your life.

Letting God Help

EXPLORATION ELEMENT: Use the evaporation of water to show kids that God wants us to open up to him so he can make us new.

BIBLE BENCHMARK: "If my people, who are called by my name, will humble themselves and pray and seek my face and turn from their wicked ways, then will I hear from heaven and will forgive their sin and will heal their land" (2 Chronicles 7:14).

SUPPLIES: You'll need a Bible, three washcloths, three resealable plastic bags or bags with twist ties, a hair dryer, and a small pitcher or cup of water. If you're not close to a sink, you'll also need a dishpan to catch any spilled water.

OPTIONAL SUPPLIES: You may want paper towels and eyedroppers or straws.

PREPARATION: Set the washcloths, the pitcher of water, and the plastic bags next to the sink. Make sure there's an outlet nearby to plug in the hair dryer.

CAUTION! Keep the hair dryer as far away as possible from the pitcher of water and the sink.

Have kids gather around the sink. Say: **I want each of you to think of three things that would be wrong for you to do. Some examples are lying to a friend, sneaking candy from your sister, or pushing a friend.** Give kids a few seconds to think, and then say: **Now I'd like you to take turns pouring a little water on each washcloth for each wrong thing you thought of. As you pour the water on**

each washcloth, say the wrong thing out loud. Make sure kids hold the washcloths over the sink while they do this. Wring out a little water if the washcloths get dripping wet.

Say: **Now we have three wet washcloths that are just like children who had very bad days. The first child does not believe in God. This child holds all her problems tightly to herself.**

Put one washcloth in a bag, and seal the bag tightly.

Say: **The next child knows about God but doesn't really ever do anything about it.**

Leave the second washcloth crumpled and laying on a table.

Say: **The third child knows God and prays to God for help and forgiveness when he makes wrong choices.**

Open the third washcloth, and spread it out on the back of a chair.

Say: **When God talks to us, it can be like a gentle wind. I have a hair dryer that will blow like God's wind.** Ask:

● **If I use the hair dryer on these three washcloths, which washcloth do you think will dry out the fastest and look like new again? Why?**

Let children take turns blowing the hair dryer on the washcloths for about two minutes. Make sure the children do not let the hair dryer touch the plastic bags or the washcloths.

After two minutes, have kids feel the washcloths. Ask:

● **Which washcloth is the driest? Why do you think that is?**

Say: **When wet washcloths have more air moving around them, the water in them will evaporate faster, and they will dry out faster.**

Read aloud 2 Chronicles 7:14, and ask:

● **According to this Bible verse, what can you do to be made new again after you've done wrong things?**

● **Which of the wet washcloths represented a child who opened himself up to God's forgiveness? Explain.**

● **What will God do for you if you pray and tell him you're sorry for your wrong choices?**

● **Why does God want you to pray to him**

Scientist's Strategy

If you want each child to have his or her own results, you may consider using paper towels. Use eyedroppers or straws to drop water on the paper towels to decrease the amount of time it will take for them to dry.

about your wrong choices?

Say: **God doesn't want you to hold your problems, mistakes, and wrong choices inside yourself; he wants you to open yourself up and share them with him. God loves you very much, and he wants to make you new. All you have to do is tell him you're sorry for your bad choices and ask for his forgiveness, and he will forgive you and make you new.**

Soak It All Up

EXPLORATION ELEMENT: Demonstrate absorption of water to show kids that faith in Jesus, rather than the works they do, is the way to a life with God.

BIBLE BENCHMARK: "Therefore, since we have been justified through faith, we have peace with God through our Lord Jesus Christ, through whom we have gained access by faith into this grace in which we now stand" (Romans 5:1-2a).

SUPPLIES: You'll need a Bible, a natural sponge and a manufactured sponge that are the same size, newspaper, four bowls that are the same size, a measuring cup, a pitcher of water, and a chalkboard and chalk or newsprint and a marker.

PREPARATION: Spread newspaper over a table or on the floor. Place the bowls, the measuring cup, and the pitcher of water on the newspaper.

Say: **We're going to do an experiment to help us understand what it means to live a Christlike life.**

I have two sponges. One is a natural sponge. Hold up the natural sponge, and say: **This sponge lived in the sea in a sponge colony. Natural sponges are usually attached to the sea floor or some other object near the sea floor. This sponge was created by God.**

Power • Heavens • Earth • Wind • Bread • Storm • Garden • Compass • Rainbow • Creati

This other sponge is a man-made sponge. Hold up the manufactured sponge, and say: **This sponge was not made by God. It was made by someone in a factory using man-made materials. During our experiment, we're going to discover if there's a difference between these two types of sponges. I'm going to pass the sponges around so you can feel them and take a closer look at them.**

After all the children have had the opportunity to see and touch the sponges, ask:

● **What did you notice that the two sponges had in common?**

● **What did you notice that was different about the two sponges?**

Have kids gather around the newspaper, and say: **I have bowls that are the same size. We're going to pour the same amount of water into two bowls.** Have two children measure and pour a cup of water into each of two bowls, and say: **Now we're going to place a sponge into each bowl.** Ask:

● **What do you think will happen?**

● **Which sponge do you think will hold the most water?**

Say: **That will be our hypothesis. A hypothesis is an educated guess using the information you already have.** Write the hypothesis (or hypotheses, if kids disagreed) on a chalkboard, and say: **Now we're ready to do our experiment to prove or disprove our hypothesis** (or hypotheses).

Have two different children place the sponges in the bowls. Watch to see what happens. Leave the sponges in the bowls for approximately three minutes. At the end of three minutes, take the sponges out of the water and place one in each of the two remaining bowls. Choose two children to squeeze all of the water out of the sponges and into the empty bowls. Make sure kids keep as much of the water in the bowls as possible. Then pour the water out of one bowl into the measuring cup to see how much water the sponge absorbed. Do the same with the second sponge. Write on a chalkboard or newsprint the amount of water each sponge held. Then read the hypothesis (or hypotheses) again. Ask:

● **Which sponge held the most water?**

● **Was our hypothesis** (or hypotheses) **correct?**

● **Why do you think the natural sponge held more water?**

Say: **Just as the sponge that God created was the best at**

ck • Light • Salt

click!

votions for Children's Ministry

absorbing water, the way God wants us to live is the best way. Ask:

- **How do you think God wants us to live?**

- **What do you think would happen if we tried to live our lives without faith in Jesus?**

Read aloud Romans 5:1-2a, and say: **This verse tells us that the best way to live the way God wants us to live is by believing in Jesus. We can't live the way God wants us to without help. We need Jesus' help to live as Christians.** Ask:

- **What do people do to try to live good lives without Jesus?**

Say: **Sometimes people think that if they are really nice to everyone or if they exactly follow all the rules, they will be living the way God wants them to live. But no matter how hard they try, they can never do enough or be good enough. The only way to be close to God is to have faith in Jesus and his death on the cross to take away our sins. God's way is the best way!**

Building an Ark

> **ExPLORATION ELEMENT:** Kids experience the effects of flotation and surface tension as they discuss the importance of exactly following God's Word.

BIBLE BENCHMARK: "So make yourself an ark of cypress wood; make rooms in it and coat it with pitch inside and out. This is how you are to build it: The ark is to be 450 feet long, 75 feet wide and 45 feet high. Make a roof for it and finish the ark to within 18 inches of the top. Put a door in the side of the ark and make lower, middle and upper decks" (Genesis 6:14–16).

SUPPLIES: You'll need a Bible, clay, a one-foot-long piece of aluminum foil for each child, newspaper, and a dishpan full of water for every four people.

PREPARATION: Spread newspaper over a table or on the floor. Place the dishpans full of water on the newspaper.

Say: **When God asked Noah to build an ark, he was very specific about how to build it.** Read Genesis 6:14-16 to the group, and then say: **Noah had to follow and obey God's Word so he would be able to make a boat that would really hold all those animals for more than 150 days.**

Have kids gather around the newspaper, and give each child a piece of aluminum foil and a small piece of clay. Say: **First I'd like you to crumple up your piece of aluminum foil into a ball and try to float it in the water.** Give kids a few moments to do this, and then ask:

● **What happened? Why do you think that happened?**

Say: **Now I'd like you to make your piece of clay into a little ball and try to float it in the water.** Give kids a few moments to do this, and then ask:

● **What happened? Why do you think that happened?**

Say: **Now I want you to follow my instructions, and we'll try to make both of these things float. First take your clay and form it into a man shape to be like Noah. Next carefully straighten out your aluminum foil, and make it into a boat shape. Put Noah into the boat, and try to make the boat float.** Ask:

● **What happened this time? Why?**

Say: **Your aluminum foil ball and your clay ball sank the first time because they had very small surface areas. This affected the water's ability to support their weight. When you spread the aluminum foil out, it made a larger surface for the water to hold up, so it was easier for the aluminum foil and the clay to float. As you saw, there was only one way to do this experiment so that** the foil and the clay would float. If you did it any other way, the foil and the clay sunk to the bottom. Ask:

● **What could have happened to Noah's ark if he had decided to change God's directions a little bit here and a little bit there?**

● **Why is it important to follow God's Word carefully?**

● **What could happen if we don't follow God's Word?**

● **Can you tell me about a time it was hard for you to follow God's Word?**

● **What is one thing you could do this week that would help you follow God's Word?**

Say: **Sometimes we may not understand God's Word, but it is very important that we listen to God and trust that he will always tell us exactly what we need to know to live for him.**

How Full Is Full?

EXPLORATION ELEMENT: Use amazing surface-tension water displays to show kids that God has more joy to share with them than they can imagine.

BIBLE BENCHMARK: "I have told you this so that my joy may be in you and that your joy may be complete" (John 15:11).

SUPPLIES: You'll need a Bible, newspaper, clear plastic cups, paper clips, a pitcher of water, and towels or paper towels.

OPTIONAL SUPPLIES: You may want envelopes or small plastic bags.

PREPARATION: Spread newspaper over a table or on the floor.

Ask:

● **Have you ever filled a glass too full? What happened?**

Say: **Today we're going to see just how full *full* really is. As we**

Power ● Heavens ● Earth ● Wind ● Bread ● Storm ● Garden ● Compass ● Rainbow ● Creati

do this experiment, I'd like you to think about how it might be like God's love for you. Have kids form groups of four, and have groups gather around the newspaper. Give each group a clear plastic cup and twenty paper clips.

Say: **Now I'll fill your cup to the rim with water without making it overflow.** Be sure to have towels on hand as you do this. After you've filled all the cups, say: **These cups are really full!** Ask:

● **What do you think would happen if you put a paper clip in the cup?**

Say: **Try it and see!** Have each group add one paper clip to its cup, and then have them continue adding paper clips, one at a time, until the water flows over the rims of the cups. Then ask:

Scientist's Strategy

You may want to separate the paper clips ahead of time and place them in envelopes.

● **How many paper clips were you able to put in the glass before the water overflowed?**

● **Why do you think we were able to put in so many paper clips before the water overflowed?**

Say: **Water molecules have a very strong attraction to each other. This makes them bond together in the cup even when it looks like the water should overflow. Because of this, adding paper clips to a full cup of water causes the water on the surface to form an upward curve.** Ask:

● **How was this a demonstration of God's love for us?**

Read aloud John 15:11, and say: **God's joy can fill us even more than we can imagine. It's easy to become content with the relationship we have with God. We must continue to seek him even when we feel filled so his joy can fill us even more.** Ask:

● **How can you continue to seek God after you've asked him to live in your heart?**

Say: **God wants to fill us and surround us with his love and joy, but he can only do that if we ask him to. Praying to God, worshiping with other Christians, and reading our Bibles are all ways we can continue to seek God and allow him to fill us up with his joy.**

Circle of Servanthood

BIBLE BENCHMARK: "I appeal to you, brothers, in the name of our Lord Jesus Christ, that all of you agree with one another so that there may be no divisions among you and that you may be perfectly united in mind and thought" (1 Corinthians 1:10).

SUPPLIES: You'll need a Bible, a six-inch length of thread, a clear glass bowl, a pitcher of water, a small bowl, liquid soap, and a toothpick.

PREPARATION: Fill the glass bowl with water (it doesn't have to be completely full), and squirt a little liquid soap in the small bowl.

Say: **We're going to do an experiment today that will show what it's like for us to work together *without* God's help. Then we'll see what it's like for us to work together *with* God's help. See if you can tell the difference.** Complete the following experiment while kids observe.

Say: **First I'll tie the ends of this piece of thread together.** Tie the ends of the thread together, and place the thread into the water. Ask:

● **What shape is the thread forming?**

● **How might this be like Christians trying to work together without God's help?**

Say: **Now I'm going to dip a toothpick into the soap. The soap represents God.** Make sure the toothpick is covered with soap, and

then place the toothpick in the middle of the thread. Ask:

- **What happened to the thread?**
- **What shape did it form?**
- **How might the smooth circle be like Christians working together with God's help?**
- **Which way would you rather work with people?**

Say: **Water molecules are attracted to each other with a powerful force. When we put the soapy toothpick into the water in the middle of the circle, it changed the attraction of the water molecules inside the circle and caused the water molecules outside the circle to tug on each other with balanced force. This made the thread form a smooth circle.**

In church, we learn that we need to work together to serve God. This is not always an easy task because sometimes we forget to let God lead us in our decisions. Read aloud 1 Corinthians 1:10, and ask:

- **Have you ever had a disagreement with someone in the church?**
- **Why are there differences between people in the church?**
- **Is it OK for there to be differences between people in the church?**

Say: **Differences between people don't have to be bad; God created us with different ideas and gifts for a reason. God wants us to use our different ideas and gifts to bring good to the church and the world. However, he wants us to work in unity as we use our ideas and gifts.** Ask:

- **What is unity?**

Say: **Unity is what happens when we all work together, with God's help, to serve God and each other.** Ask:

- **What will unity do for the church?**

Say: **Let's always remember to ask God to lead us and work with us so we can have unity in our church and in our lives.**

Friends Stick Together

BIBLE BENCHMARK: "A man of many companions may come to ruin, but there is a friend who sticks closer than a brother" (Proverbs 18:24).

SUPPLIES: You'll need a Bible, two pieces of paper for each child, pens, various stackable plastic containers, paper plates, at least two stackable plastic drinking glasses, and a few spray bottles full of water.

PREPARATION: None is needed.

Give each child two pieces of paper and a pen, and say: **I'd like you to draw pictures of some things a friend has done or said that made you angry.** Give kids a few minutes to do this, and then say: **See if you can get your two pieces of paper to stick together without folding them. It doesn't work, does it? Sometimes when a friend says or does mean things to us, we don't want to be that person's friend anymore. We want to walk away from him or her.**

Give a few kids the spray bottles, and say: **Now I'd like you to take turns spraying a little water on your pieces of paper. After you've done that, try to get them to stick together.** Give kids a few minutes to do this, and then ask:

● **Did it work? Why do you think that is?**

Invite kids to repeat the experiment with the plastic containers, the plastic drinking glasses, or the paper plates. Ask:

● **Why do you think these things stayed apart when they were dry but stuck together when they were wet?**

Say: **The pieces of paper, the plastic containers, and the paper plates stuck together when they were wet because the molecules in water are very attracted to each other, so they stick together really well.** Ask:

● **Can you think of a time you had to stick by a friend? Tell me about it.**

Read aloud Proverbs 18:24, and then say: **Just as the pieces of paper and the other things stuck to each other, God wants us to stick by our friends even when they say or do mean things to us. The next time one of your friends does something mean to you, try to remember this Bible verse.** Ask:

● **What are some things you could do to stick by a friend?**

● **What could happen if you don't stick by a friend?**

Say: **When we stick by our friends even though bad things are threatening to pull us away from them, we are showing our friends what God is like. God is the best friend of all, and he sticks by us no matter what.**

Parting the Red Sea

ExPLORATION ELEMENT: Kids see that soap weakens water's bonding properties as they explore that God's power helps us to trust him.

BIBLE BENCHMARK: "And when the Israelites saw the great power the Lord displayed against the Egyptians, the people feared the Lord and put their trust in him and in Moses his servant" (Exodus 14:31).

SUPPLIES: You'll need a Bible, newspaper, several cups or bowls, a pitcher of water, red food coloring, pepper and other dark-colored spices, and liquid soap.

PREPARATION: Spread newspaper over a table or on the floor. Place the cups or bowls and the pitcher of water on the newspaper.

Tell the story of Moses parting the Red Sea or read the account found in Exodus 14 before beginning this activity.

Have kids gather around the newspaper, and say: **The Israelites really needed a safe way to cross the Red Sea. They couldn't do it**

without God's help.

Pour water into one of the cups, and add red food coloring to the water. Then sprinkle pepper on top of the water.

Let kids try to use their fingers or their breath to make a clear area in the bowl.

After kids try several techniques, say: **The Israelites needed God's help, and it looks like we need some help, too.** Put a small drop of liquid soap on each child's finger, and have children touch the water again. Ask:

● **What happened when you put your soapy finger in the water?**

● **How did it feel when the pepper spread away?**

● **How do you think the Israelites felt when the Red Sea parted for them?**

Fill other bowls with water, and let kids try the same experiment with other spices. Ask:

● **Do you always get the same results?**

● **Why do the spices move away from your finger when it has soap on it and not when it's clean?**

Say: **Water molecules are very attracted to each other, and they create a strong bond with each other. The spices we put in the bowls floated on top of the water's bond. Soap weakens the water molecules' bond with each other; when the bond is weakened, the spices move with the water. The soap in this experiment is kind of like God's power when he parted the Red Sea. God can do anything; we just need to trust him.** Read aloud Exodus 14:31, and ask:

- **How did the Israelites respond when God parted the Red Sea?**
- **Do you think God will be there to help you if you need help?**
- **What is something God could help you do?**
- **How can you get help from God during this next week?**

Say: **When you see God's power displayed in the world around you, it can help you to know that you can trust God with everything in your life and he will take care of you.**

We Live Through Him

EXPLORATION ELEMENT: Use water's bonding properties and gravity to show kids that God's blessings are constant.

BIBLE BENCHMARK: "This is how God showed his love among us: He sent his one and only Son into the world that we might live through him" (1 John 4:9).

SUPPLIES: You'll need a Bible, newspaper, water in a small pitcher that has a spout, a wide-mouthed container, and a three-foot piece of cotton string.

PREPARATION: Spread newspaper over a table or on the floor. Place the pitcher of water and the wide-mouthed container on the newspaper.

sk:

- **What kinds of blessings does God give to his children?**

Say: **We're going to do an experiment today that will help us see more about how God wants to bless his children.**

Have kids gather around the newspaper. Dip the piece of string into the water in the pitcher, and tie one end of the string to the pitcher's handle. Pull the wet string through the pitcher's spout and over to the empty container. Let the free end drop into the container. (See the illustration.)

wer * Heavens * Earth * Wind * Bread * Storm * Garden * Compass * Rainbow * Creation

Carefully pour the water into the container so the water runs down the wet string. Ask:

● **Why do you think the water slides down the string?**

Say: **The water slides down the string because the molecules that form water are very attracted to each other. This makes them stick together. The force of gravity makes them move down the string together. And as long as I'm pouring water from the pitcher, the water will travel down the string this way.**

● **How is this like what God does when he gives you blessings?**

Say: **Just like the water continues to flow down the string, God gives you blessings constantly because he loves you.** Ask:

● **What do you think will happen if I pour the water too fast?**

Pour the water faster and see what happens. Ask:

● **Does God ever give you too many blessings?**

Say: **God always gives you just the right number of blessings because he knows what you need.** Ask:

● **What was the biggest blessing God ever gave us?**

Read aloud 1 John 4:9, and say: **Because God loves us so much, he gave us the blessing of his Son to take away our sins.** Ask:

● **How can you thank God for the blessings he gives you?**

Say: **God gives us so many things because we're special to him. He sent his Son to die so that we can live forever with him. We can thank God by praying to him, worshiping him, and being the "string" that carries his goodness to the people around us.**

Power ● Heavens ● Earth ● Wind ● Bread ● Storm ● Garden ● Compass ● Rainbow ● Creat

arden of God's Goodness

EXPLORATION ELEMENT: Use this experiment, which demonstrates a chemical reaction that turns something ugly into something beautiful, to show kids God can make good come from bad things in their lives.

BIBLE BENCHMARK: "And we know that in all things God works for the good of those who love him" (Romans 8:28a).

SUPPLIES: You'll need a Bible, newspaper, two or three porous rocks, five or six pieces of charcoal, a measuring cup, ammonia, salt, liquid bluing (found in the laundry aisle of a supermarket), food coloring (any color), a shallow bowl or a baking pan, a mixing bowl, and a metal spoon.

OPTIONAL SUPPLIES: You may need a container of water.

PREPARATION: Spread newspaper over a table or on the floor. Place the items to be used in the experiment on the newspaper.

Read aloud Romans 8:28a, and say: **Let's do a "science play" that will show us what this verse is saying.** Hold up the porous rocks, and say: **These rocks are to remind us of hard times we go through.** Ask:

- **Can anybody think of an example of a hard time? Explain.**

Have a child put the rocks in the shallow bowl, and set it aside. Hold up the charcoal, and say: **This charcoal is to remind us of dark times that make us feel sad.** Ask:

- **Can any of you think of a time you were sad? Explain.**

Have a child put the charcoal in the shallow bowl.

Say: **These rocks and charcoal are not very pretty to look at. Hard times and dark times are not very fun.**

Let's pretend that the ammonia represents God's power because ammonia has such a strong smell. Measure one-fourth cup of ammonia, and pour it into the mixing bowl.

Say: **Now let's pretend that the salt is God's protection. Salt is used to keep food from going bad, and God's protection keeps things from happening that are too much for us to handle.** Have a volunteer measure and pour one-fourth cup of salt into the mixing bowl. Say: **The liquid bluing represents God's love because God is a true-blue friend.** Have a volunteer measure and add one-fourth cup of liquid bluing to the mixing bowl. Say: **The food coloring is like God's imagination. God loves to create, and he adds color and beauty to anything he touches.** Have a volunteer squirt in several drops of food coloring, and then have another volunteer carefully mix the ingredients together. Have a third volunteer pour the mixture over the rocks and charcoal in the shallow bowl. Have the group watch to see what happens. Ask:

Scientist's Strategy

Ammonia can be a dangerous substance! If kids get any on their skin, be sure to have them wash it thoroughly.

● **What do you see happening to the rocks and the charcoal?**

● **How would you describe what grew out of the rocks and the charcoal?**

Say: **The mixture of ingredients combined with the charcoal created a chemical reaction and made energy. The charcoal is made out of carbon. The energy from the chemical reaction makes carbon change shapes. The shape the carbon is now in is called a crystal.** Ask:

● **What does this experiment tell you about what God can do with your hard and sad times?**

● **Does God always make hard times better as fast as the carbon crystallized?**

● **Did the rocks and charcoal disappear?**

Say: **God has the power to change hard and sad situations into something beautiful. Sometimes he does not take the "rocky" times away completely, but he always helps us grow through them. You can trust that God is strong enough to turn bad things into good and that he can work through everything in your life.**

Changing Shapes

BIBLE BENCHMARK: "Do not conform any longer to the pattern of this world, but be transformed by the renewing of your mind. Then you will be able to test and approve what God's will is—his good, pleasing and perfect will" (Romans 12:2).

SUPPLIES: You'll need a Bible, a measuring cup, measuring spoons, a container of water, cornstarch, a mixing bowl, a spoon, food coloring, clear containers of assorted sizes and shapes, and washcloths.

PREPARATION: None is needed.

Read aloud Romans 12:2 to the group. Ask:

● **Does God want you to try to be just like other people? Why or why not?**

Say: **We're going to try an experiment that will show how a substance is distributed to fit the shape of the container it is poured into. This experiment can help us understand that God doesn't want us to be like other people; he wants us to pattern our lives after him.**

Make "goop" by following these instructions: Have one volunteer measure one-half cup of cornstarch into the mixing bowl. Have a second volunteer measure one-fourth cup plus one tablespoon of water into the bowl, and then ask a third volunteer to stir the mixture. The goop will be difficult to stir, but encourage the child to keep stirring! Have another volunteer add a few drops of food coloring to the mixture, and have the first child keep stirring until the mixture appears to be homogeneous. Ask:

● **Why do you think the goop is difficult to stir?**

● **Did you think it would mix together easily?**

Pour the goop mixture into one container, making sure that the amount you pour into that container will fit into the other containers as well. Then ask:

- **What shape is the goop now?**

Have a child pour the goop from the first container into a different container. Ask:

- **Is the goop still the same shape? What shape is it now?**

Let kids take turns trying this with all the containers you have available. Ask:

- **What happens when we pour a substance like goop from one container to another?**

- **Why do you think the goop takes on the shape of each container it's in?**

Let kids handle the goop mixture. Ask:

- **What does it feel like to hold the goop?**

- **How does it change when you hold it? What happens to it?**

Give kids washcloths to clean up their goopy hands, and say: **The scientific word for the way liquids change their shape to fit into different spaces is "distribution." When the goop mixture is mixed, the molecules are in a state of suspension. This means the molecules in the water are holding up the cornstarch molecules. When you squeeze the mixture together, it feels solid; but when you stop squeezing, the solid and the liquid separate.**

In Romans, we read that God wants us to live a different life from people who don't believe in him. Because you love God and you are loved by God in return, you can be a new person. We know that when we pour a substance from one container to another, it's exactly the same amount of the same substance, but it has a different shape. In the same way, when you ask God to lead your life and try to follow him, you're still the same person, but God changes your shape and makes you more like him.

Scientist's Strategy

If you have enough supplies, this is a fun project for groups of two to four kids to work on together and see if they get the same result. Remember: Food coloring can stain hands, clothing, and table tops.

Problem Solvers

EXPLORATION ELEMENT: Kids try to solve a problem and explore how we can find God's solutions to our problems.

BIBLE BENCHMARKS: "To these four young men God gave knowledge and understanding" (Daniel 1:17a).

"If any of you lacks wisdom, he should ask God, who gives generously to all without finding fault, and it will be given to him" (James 1:5).

SUPPLIES: You'll need a Bible, newspaper, six clear plastic cups for each group of four or five kids, a pitcher of water, and a permanent marker.

PREPARATION: Around each cup, draw a line about an inch from the bottom to show how full to fill it.

Before beginning this activity, tell the story of Daniel's refusal to eat the king's food, or read the account found in Daniel 1. Then read aloud Daniel 1:17a to the group.

Say: **Daniel and his friends had a big problem, didn't they? We're going to do an experiment today that shows us what Daniel and his friends did to solve their problem.**

Have kids get into groups of four or five, and give each group six cups and some newspaper. Say: **Now I'd like you to spread your newspaper on a table or the floor and set your cups out on top of it. I'll come around and fill three of your cups with water.** Fill three of each group's cups with water to the lines you drew before class, and leave three of each group's cups empty. Then say: **Place your cups in a straight line in this pattern: two empty cups, three full cups, and one empty cup.**

Now I'd like you to try to change the order your cups are in to make this pattern: one full, one empty, one full, one empty, one full, and one empty. The only rule is that you can only move one cup.

Let groups work for a few minutes to try to solve the problem, and then ask:

• Did anyone figure it out?

Say: **Let me give you the solution: The way to create the pattern is by pouring the water from the fourth cup into the first cup and then putting the fourth cup back where it was.**

It was very difficult to find the solution to this problem. I could see that some of you were feeling frustrated because you didn't know the answer and you didn't know how to find the solution. Daniel and his friends may not have known where to find God's answer to their problem at first, either. Ask:

• When someone has a question about God, where can that person go to find the answer?

Say: **God has given us a wonderful source of information in his Word, the Holy Bible. The Bible is a gift from God that we can use to find answers and solutions to tough questions and problems. Daniel and his friends used God's rules to help them solve their problem; they chose to follow God's rules even though the king wanted them to do something else. And as we saw, God helped them solve the problem. Sometimes you may have difficult questions about God or may have problems understanding God, too.** Ask:

• What problems have you faced in your life?

• How did you know what to do to solve the problem?

Read aloud James 1:5, and say: **God wants to help us solve our problems through his Word. We can learn more about God by following his Word just as Daniel and his friends did.**

Amazing Science

Ministry • Rock • Light • Salt • Living Wate

God Moves in Mysterious Ways

EXPLORATION ELEMENT: Experiment with the principle of inertia to help kids understand God's power.

BIBLE BENCHMARK: "Go, gather together all the Jews who are in Susa, and fast for me. Do not eat or drink for three days, night or day. I and my maids will fast as you do. When this is done, I will go to the king, even though it is against the law. And if I perish, I perish" (Esther 4:16).

SUPPLIES: You'll need a Bible, a chair with wheels, and three or four large books such as dictionaries.

OPTIONAL SUPPLIES: You may want windup toys.

PREPARATION: Stack the large books on the seat of the chair with wheels.

Tell the story of Esther before beginning this activity. Then read aloud Esther 4:16. Say: **Esther took quite a risk, didn't she? Today we're going to do an experiment that will help us understand some of the amazing ways God displays his power.**

Bring out the chair with wheels, and ask for a volunteer. Ask the class:

• **What do you think will happen to these books if my volunteer moves the chair forward really fast and then stops it? Why?**

Have the volunteer try this. The books will keep moving after the chair stops, and they'll fall off the chair onto the floor. Ask:

• **Why didn't the books stop when the chair stopped?**

• **When did they finally stop?**

Scientist's Strategy

For further experimentation with inertia, let kids play with windup toys and then discuss how the mechanical power of the toys overcomes the natural force of inertia.

ower * Heavens * Earth * Wind * Bread * Storm * Garden * Compass * Rainbow * Creation

- What stopped them?

Say: **Nothing starts moving or stops moving in God's universe unless something makes it move or stop moving. This property of matter is called "inertia." Everything in the universe is made of matter. If something moves, it's because something else has pushed or pulled it. It will keep moving until something else acts upon it to stop it.**

We push and pull ourselves to get out of bed, to go to school, to kick a ball, to write a sentence, to type on a computer, or to tie our shoes. Inertia has another meaning, too. It also means "inactivity." Esther could have been overcome by inertia and chosen not to act, but instead, she acted. Esther overcame inertia to confront the king. The inertia she overcame was both physical and mental. She dared to act when others wouldn't. The king's heart would not have been moved if Esther hadn't confronted him. Esther was armed with her faith in God. Ask:

- **Can you think of a time you overcame your own inertia and did something positive? Explain.**

- **What helps you act in spite of your tendency toward inertia?**

Say: **Your service to God conquers inertia. Going to church, praying, doing service projects, and helping others defeats the inertia of not doing anything at all. Every once in a while, God gives us a little push to overcome our tendencies to do nothing. If we follow his lead, God can give us the power to do great things for him!**

Power • Heavens • Earth •   • Garden • Compass • Rainbow • Creati

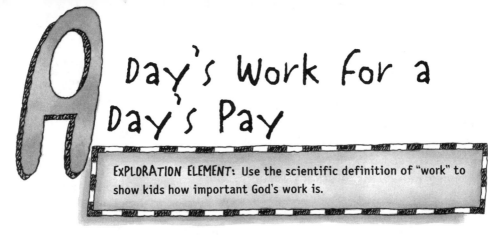

Day's Work for a Day's Pay

EXPLORATION ELEMENT: Use the scientific definition of "work" to show kids how important God's work is.

BIBLE BENCHMARK: "For the Scripture says, 'Do not muzzle the ox while it is treading out the grain,' and 'The worker deserves his wages' " (1 Timothy 5:18).

SUPPLIES: You'll need a Bible and paper clips.

PREPARATION: None is needed.

Say: **Today we're going to talk a little bit about work.** Ask:
- **What comes to mind when I say the word "work"?**

Let kids give a few answers, and then read aloud 1 Timothy 5:18. Ask:
- **What do you think this verse means?**

Say: **The Apostle Paul wrote these words to his friend Timothy to remind him that the quality of the work a person puts out should be rewarded appropriately. A person who does a good day's work should get paid for it, although he or she may not always get paid in money. A person who puts no time or effort into good works or hard work should get paid little or none. You see it yourselves on report cards: Quality work gets better grades. Little or no work earns lower grades. The best rewards are achieved when care is taken with what you have to do.**

Science explains the word "work" differently from how we do. Work takes place when force is applied to an object and the object moves. Have kids line up facing one solid wall, and say: **On the count of three, I'd like you to try to move this wall. One, two, three!** Let kids push against the wall for a few seconds, and then ask:
- **Was that hard work? Explain.**
- **The wall didn't move, did it? According to the definition of**

work I just gave you, did you do any work?

Say: **Scientifically speaking, when you push against a wall and the wall doesn't move, you haven't done any work. You could push harder, sweat, and grunt and groan, and that stubborn wall still won't move. You still haven't done any work!**

Set a paper clip in front of each child, and say: **Now on the count of three, I'd like you to try to make the paper clip move. One, two, three!**

Let kids move their paper clips, and then ask:

Scientist's Strategy

If you'd like to expand this idea a bit further, have kids role play parts of different jobs of the era. Ask them about the work, or lack of work, being done, according to the laws of physics.

● **That was pretty easy, wasn't it? According to the scientific definition of work, did you do any work?**

Say: **According to the laws of science, moving that paper clip was work, but pushing hard against the wall wasn't work. Your muscles might not agree, though!**

Work in Jesus' day was hard labor for the working class. They were farmers, carpenters, sailors, shepherds, and ordinary laborers who worked long days. The working class during that time was paid mostly in goods rather than money. A worker might get eggs for wood, a tool for a lamb, or a woven rug for water rights. If these laborers didn't work hard, they might starve, so hard work was valued even more than money. Ask:

● **What kind of work did Jesus do besides carpentry?**

Say: **Jesus did God's work on earth. He brought us the good news of God's amazing love and grace, and he taught people to love one another. It was a different kind of work from what people of that day might have been used to, but it was the most important work of all. Instead of moving objects, Jesus moved people!** Ask:

● **How much work does it take to do the will of God?**
● **What kind of work is it for you to obey the Bible?**
● **When is it work for you to love another person?**
● **What are other ways you can do the work of God?**

Say: **Think about the work you do every day, and remember that doing God's work is the most blessed and honorable job of all!**

Power ● Heavens ● Storm ● Garden ● Compass ● Rainbow ● Creatio

Holy Spirit "Hovercraft"

> **EXPLORATION ELEMENT:** Show how air pressure can briefly overcome the force of gravity as you help kids discover the power of the Holy Spirit.

BIBLE BENCHMARK: "And I will ask the Father, and he will give you another Counselor to be with you forever—the Spirit of truth" (John 14:16-17a).

SUPPLIES: You'll need a Bible; an empty, clean, twenty-ounce, plastic soft drink bottle with its cap; sharp scissors; a drill with a one-eighth-inch bit; and a large balloon.

OPTIONAL SUPPLIES: You may want extra supplies so kids can create their own "Hovercrafts."

PREPARATION: Cut off the top inch of the soft drink bottle (including the bottle cap) with the scissors. Drill a hole in the top of the bottle cap, and then screw the cap back onto the bottle.

Read aloud John 14:16-17a, and say: **We're going to do an experiment that can help us understand this passage. Let's pretend that this bottle top represents you.** Ask:

● **Can you make this bottle top float over the table? Why not?**

Say: **One of the forces that keeps the bottle top on the table is gravity. Gravity is the force that pulls everything toward the center of the earth. It's what keeps things "stuck" to the ground. We may want the bottle top to travel, but it can't because gravity keeps it stuck to the table. You and I are**

Scientist's Strategy

The rim of the bottle top must be perfectly flat. If it's not, air will escape without making a cushion of air, and the "Hovercraft" will not float. This may take a few attempts to get just right, but it's worth it!

kind of like the bottle top; we may want to follow Jesus and do whatever he tells us to do, but sometimes we get stuck. Ask:

• **What kinds of things make us stuck and keep us from following God the way we want to?**

• **Do you think God wants us to stay stuck?**

• **How does God help us get unstuck?**

Say: **Let's see what happens when the power of the wind goes through the bottle top.** Have a volunteer blow up the balloon and pinch its neck so air can't escape. Then have a second student stretch the mouth of the balloon over the bottle top. After the balloon is stretched tightly over the cap, have the child let go of the balloon, and then have him or her gently push the "Hovercraft." Ask:

• **What happened when you pushed the "Hovercraft"?**

• **Why do you think this happened?**

Say: **The force of the wind coming out of the balloon was stronger than gravity, and it** lifted the bottle top on a cushion of air. The verse we read says Jesus asked God to send us a helper called the Holy Spirit. In the Bible, the Holy Spirit sometimes acted like the wind (Acts 2). We can't see the Holy Spirit, but we can feel the work he does. Ask:

For maximum participation, create enough "Hovercrafts" for each child to have one.

• **How is the wind going through the bottle top like the Holy Spirit working in our lives?**

• **What are some things we need the Holy Spirit's power to help us do this week?**

Say: **We may want to follow God and do everything he wants us to do, but we can't do it by ourselves. We keep getting ourselves stuck by not always obeying God. God loves us enough to help us get unstuck. He forgives us when we disobey him, and he gives us his helper called the Holy Spirit. The Holy Spirit also gives us the power to obey God. We can ask God to let the Holy Spirit give us the power to obey him.**

Rolling Uphill?

EXPLORATION ELEMENT: Use an object's center of gravity to show kids that God's way is the only right way.

BIBLE BENCHMARK: "There is a way that seems right to a man, but in the end it leads to death" (Proverbs 14:12).

SUPPLIES: You'll need a Bible, two stacks of books (one about six inches high and the other about one foot high), two yardsticks, two funnels (they need to be the same size), and masking tape.

PREPARATION: Set the two stacks of books about thirty inches apart on the floor. Make a "track" by taping the two yardsticks together across one end. Put the taped end on the short stack of books. Spread the yardsticks out, and put the other ends on the taller stack of books. Make a "car" by taping the two funnels together at the large end.

Ask:
- **Are you ever in situations in which you feel pressured to do the wrong thing? Explain.**
- **How do you make the right decision?**

Say: **Today we're going to do an experiment that shows us that sometimes wrong decisions might appear to be right.**

wer • Heavens • Earth • Wind • Bread • Storm • Garden • Compass • Rainbow • Creation

Have kids gather around the stacks of books, and say: **I'm going to put my car** (hold up the funnels) **on this track close to the shorter stack of books.** Ask:

- **What do you think will happen? Why?**

Set the car on the track close to the shorter stack of books, and let the car go. It should move toward the taller stack of books. Ask:

- **What happened?**
- **Why do you think the car moved up?**
- **Do you think the car really moved up?**

Say: **No, the car didn't really move up. Gravity always pulls things down, so it's impossible for the car to move up. Why did the car look like it was rolling uphill? Let's try it again. This time, I'd like you to watch from the side to see what is happening.** Set the car on the bottom of the track again, and let it go. Say: **Did you notice that as the track got wider and wider, the center of the car got lower and lower? The car was really moving downhill. It only** *appeared* **to roll uphill.** Ask:

- **How is this like bad choices in our lives that sometimes seem like the right decisions?**

Read aloud Proverbs 14:12, and say: **Sometimes what we want—or our way—seems right. After all, it may seem that everyone is doing it that way! But God's way is the only correct way. Pressure to do the wrong thing sometimes may feel very strong, but remember: Only God's way is right. Things aren't always as they seem!** Roll the car again as a reminder.

Scientist's Strategy

The kids might like to experiment with other heights to see what they do to the center of gravity.

Power • Heavens • Earth • Wind • Bread • Storm • Garden • Compass • Rainbow • Creat

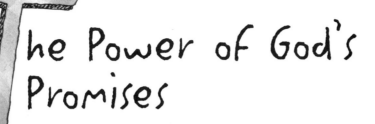

The Power of God's Promises

EXPLORATION ELEMENT: Compare the strength of reinforced cardboard to the strength our faith can have when it's reinforced with prayer.

BIBLE BENCHMARK: "I tell you the truth, if you have faith as small as a mustard seed, you can say to this mountain, 'Move from here to there' and it will move. Nothing will be impossible for you" (Matthew 17:20b).

SUPPLIES: You'll need a Bible, two 4x12-inch strips of corrugated cardboard, one twelve-ounce frozen juice can, two heavy books such as dictionaries, and masking tape or rubber bands.

PREPARATION: None is needed.

sk:
• **Can you think of any Bible stories in which people weren't sure they believed God's Word?**
• **Can you think of any people today who aren't sure they believe God's Word?**

Say: **Even Jesus' disciples sometimes were afraid and weren't sure they trusted Jesus.** Ask:
• **Have you ever been afraid and failed to trust Jesus?**

Say: **Today we're going to do an experiment which will help us see that Jesus can make us strong.** Have a child help you wrap the piece of corrugated cardboard around the juice can, and let another child wrap masking tape around the cardboard to keep it firmly in place. Slide the juice can out of the cardboard.

Say: **Jesus' words are powerful!** Read aloud Matthew 17:20b to the students, and say: **Wow! That's pretty amazing, isn't it?** Ask:
• **Have you ever been in a situation in which Jesus' words gave you strength?**

- **What is the strongest thing you can think of?**
- **How strong do you think this cardboard is? Do you think it's strong enough for a book to sit on?**

Say: **Well, let's find out!** Give one volunteer a heavy book and the piece of flat cardboard, and say: **I'd like you to try to hold up your piece of cardboard on one edge on the table** (or the floor) **and then try to balance the book on top.** Give the child a few seconds to do this, and then ask:

- **Did it work? Why not?**
- **Do you think the cardboard tube is strong enough for a book to sit on?**

Give a second volunteer the cardboard tube and a heavy book, and say: **I'd like you to try to balance the book on top of the cardboard tube.** Ask:

- **Did that work? Why?**
- **Which is stronger: the cardboard piece or the tube? Why?**

Say: **Cardboard is a strong material. But cardboard is even stronger when we form it in a different shape and reinforce it with masking tape** (or rubber bands), **as we did with this tube.** Ask:

- **How is this like God's Word and pro-mises?**

Say: **The Word and promises of God are strong and powerful, too. They have even more power in your life when you shape your life the way God wants you to and reinforce your life with faith and prayer.** Ask:

Scientist's Strategy

Older students would enjoy doing this experiment in pairs.

- **What can you do to shape your life in a way that will make God happy?**
- **What are good ways to reinforce your faith in God?**

Say: **The next time your faith feels kind of weak and you're not sure if you believe God's Word, remember this experiment: You may need to shape your life a little differently and reinforce it with prayer.**

Poppin' With Joy

EXPLORATION ELEMENT: Compare the "pop" that results from corn's exposure to pressure to ways we can "burst" with the joy of God's love.

BIBLE BENCHMARK: "Shout for joy to the Lord, all the earth. Worship the Lord with gladness; come before him with joyful songs. Know that the Lord is God. It is he who made us, and we are his; we are his people, the sheep of his pasture. Enter his gates with thanksgiving and his courts with praise; give thanks to him and praise his name. For the Lord is good and his love endures forever; his faithfulness continues through all generations" (Psalm 100).

SUPPLIES: You'll need a Bible, an air popcorn-popper, unpopped corn (check the popcorn popper's instructions for the correct amount), an extension cord (if needed), and a large tablecloth or a blanket.

OPTIONAL SUPPLIES: You may want butter, salt, napkins, and paper bowls or cups.

PREPARATION: Spread the tablecloth on the floor, and set the popcorn popper in the center.

Scientist's Strategy

You might want to have extra popcorn flavored with butter and salt to make and eat! It's always fun to try an experiment that has such tasty results.

Ask:

• **When you are excited or happy, what do you do?**

Read aloud Psalm 100 to the group, and say: **The psalmist wrote this psalm as a way of praising and thanking God because he was so happy that God loved him. This experiment might help us understand how we can show our happiness, too!**

Have kids sit around the edges of the tablecloth. Pour the unpopped corn into the popcorn popper, and turn on the machine. (Be sure to leave the lid off.) As the machine warms up, ask:

• **What do you think is happening to the popcorn right now?**

• **Why does corn pop?**

• **Can you think of a time you felt so happy or excited that you thought you might burst? Explain.**

Once the corn starts popping, the fun begins! As the corn pops all over the tablecloth, everyone will want to try to catch and "test" a few pieces! Be sure kids are at a safe distance from the popper so kernels won't hit them.

Once the corn has popped, turn off the machine, and say: **There's a scientific word to explain why the corn pops: pressure. Pressure is a pushing force. Each of these corn kernels has moisture inside. As the kernel heats up, steam is created inside the kernel. The steam puts pressure on the outside layer of the kernel, and eventually it bursts! Not all of the kernels pop open, though. See the unpopped corn kernels?** Show kids any kernels that haven't popped, and then say: **A kernel that has a little crack in it or that is dried out** won't pop because the moisture inside it can escape easily.

When you know that God loves you and that Jesus died so you might have a full life, you can get so excited and filled with joy that you practically burst, too! Ask:

- Just as the popcorn pops, how can you "burst" with God's love?

Say: Sometimes your smile, your laugh, or just the way you share love can be an expression of the excitement you have because you know you're loved by God. When people around you see you "bursting" with God's love, they will want to know more about God!

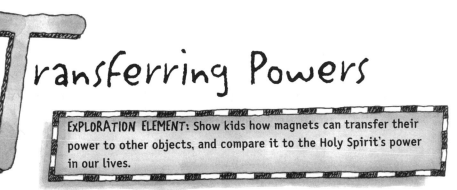

Transferring Powers

EXPLORATION ELEMENT: Show kids how magnets can transfer their power to other objects, and compare it to the Holy Spirit's power in our lives.

BIBLE BENCHMARK: "But you will receive power when the Holy Spirit comes on you" (Acts 1:8a).

SUPPLIES: You'll need a Bible, a steel knitting needle, a large bar magnet, and a box of paper clips.

OPTIONAL SUPPLIES: You may want paper, pencils, and extra knitting needles and magnets.

PREPARATION: None is needed.

Say: Today we're going to learn about magnets and transferring magnetic powers. Give one child the knitting needle and a paper clip, and ask him or her to try to pick up the paper clip with the knitting needle without running the tip of the needle through one of the holes in the paper clip. Ask:

wer * Heavens * Earth * Wind * Bread * Storm * Garden * Compass * Rainbow * Creation

- **Why couldn't you pick up the paper clip?**

Ask another child to try to pick up a paper clip with the magnet. Ask:

- **Why did the magnet pick up the paper clip?**
- **What could we do to make the knitting needle have the power to attract the clip?**

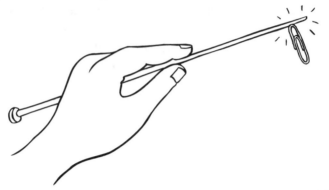

Show the kids how to magnetize the knitting needle: Hold the knitting needle near the top, and stroke it with one side of the magnet slowly and firmly. Be sure to move the magnet in one direction only, and move it from the middle of the needle to its tip. Do this about ten times. Choose another volunteer, and give him or her the magnetized knitting needle and a paper clip. Say: **Now try to pick up the paper clip with the needle.** (If the knitting needle doesn't hold the paper clip, do another ten strokes.) Ask:

- **What happened? Why?**

Say: **Let's see how many paper clips the knitting needle can pick up.** Have another volunteer stroke the knitting needle with the magnet another ten to twenty times. Choose someone else to see how many paper clips the knitting needle will pick up. Ask:

- **What do you notice now?**

Say: **The more the knitting needle is exposed to the magnet, the more power it has. This reminds me of our lives as Christians.**

Scientist's Strategy

For maximum participation, have kids form pairs, and give each pair a magnet, a knitting needle, and some paper clips. One child in each pair can magnetize the knitting needle, and the other child can record the number of paper clips that can be picked up. The kids can then alternate jobs until the knitting needle isn't charged anymore.

Read aloud Acts 1:8a, and then ask:

● **What does this Scripture tell us about God's power?**

Say: **The Scripture says you'll receive power when the Holy Spirit comes to you.** Ask:

● **How is this like the power of the magnet on the knitting needle?**

Say: **The power of the Spirit is transferred to you like the power of the magnet was transferred to the knitting needle. The knitting needle had no power on its own; it only had the power it received from the magnet. In the same way, you have no power without the Holy Spirit in your life. Did you notice that the more the knitting needle was exposed to the power of the magnet, the more power the knitting needle had?** Ask:

● **How is this like your life as a Christian?**

Say: **Greater exposure to the magnet gave the knitting needle more power. In the same way, the more you study the Bible and pray, the more you will learn to rely on the Holy Spirit and let God's power work in your life!**

Scientist's Strategy

You can demagnetize the knitting needle by whacking it against the edge of a desk several times or by holding the knitting needle in a flame until it gets very hot and then plunging it into cold water. Repeat both procedures if necessary. (Do this before taking the knitting needle home next to your cassette tapes!)

Your Compass for Life

EXPLORATION ELEMENT: Use a magnet to make a compass as you help kids explore God's compass for their lives, the Bible.

BIBLE BENCHMARK: "Do your best to present yourself to God as one approved, a workman who does not need to be ashamed and who correctly handles the word of truth" (2 Timothy 2:15).

ock ● Light ● Salt ● Living Water ● Amazing Science Devotions for Children's Ministry

SUPPLIES: You'll need a Bible, a needle, a bar magnet, a straight pin, an empty margarine tub, a cork (about one-fourth-inch thick), a pitcher of water, and liquid dish soap.

OPTIONAL SUPPLIES: You may want extra supplies for kids to make their own compasses.

PREPARATION: None is needed.

sk:

- **Have any of you ever been sailing?**
- **What do sailors use to steer their ships in the right direction?**

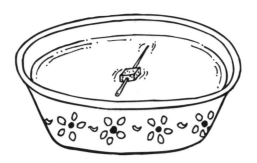

Say: **A compass is probably the most important tool a sailor has. Before the days of radar and radios, a compass and the stars were all sailors had to tell them if they were on the right path. Today we're going to make a compass. I'm going to start by magnetizing my needle, or making my needle attract other metal objects.** Magnetize the needle by rubbing one end of the bar magnet over the needle about forty times. Be sure to always use the same end of the magnet and to stroke the needle in the same direction. Say: **Now I'll test the needle to see if it's been magnetized.** To test the needle, try to pick up the straight pin with it. Then say: **Now I'm going to poke the needle into the cork so that the needle will float.** Poke the needle through the cork from side to side, not from top to bottom. The needle should stick out from the cork quite a bit on each side. Then say: **Now I'll fill my container with water and add a little soap.** Fill the margarine tub half full of water, and add a few drops of liquid dish soap. Then say: **Now I'm going to float the cork in the water. Watch what happens when I turn the container around.** Ask:

● **What do you notice about the needle when I turn the container?**

● **Why does the needle keep pointing in the same direction?**

● **What direction does it point?**

Say: **A compass needle always points to the north. You can always depend on that. Sailors can depend on their compasses to give them an accurate reading.** Ask:

● **What can we depend on in our lives to keep us on the right track?** Read aloud 2 Timothy 2:15. Ask:

● **What is the "word of truth" the Scripture is talking about here?**

● **How can you learn to correctly handle the word of truth?**

Say: **All the directions for your life are in the Bible, but if you don't read it, you won't know which way to go. The Word of God is what keeps you on the right path just as a compass keeps sailors on the right path. The Bible—God's Word of truth—is our compass for life.**

Follow the Path

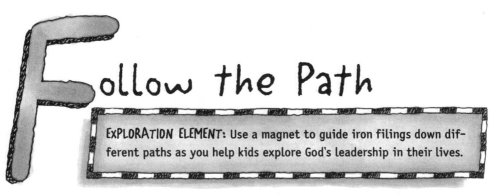

EXPLORATION ELEMENT: Use a magnet to guide iron filings down different paths as you help kids explore God's leadership in their lives.

BIBLE BENCHMARK: "You have made known to me the path of life; you will fill me with joy in your presence, with eternal pleasures at your right hand" (Psalm 16:11).

Heavens * Earth * Wind * Bread * Storm * Garden * Compass * Rainbo

SUPPLIES: You'll need a Bible, an overhead projector, two plastic transparency sheets, a permanent marker, a magnet or a magnet wand, and iron filings.

PREPARATION: Set up the overhead projector close to an electrical outlet.

Open your Bible to the book of Psalms, and read aloud Psalm 16:11 to the group. Say: **It isn't always easy to know what to do, but God has promised always to show us the right way to go. This experiment is a fun way to help us see that God can guide us through every day!**

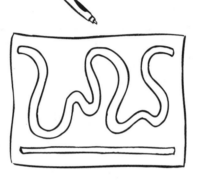

Have kids gather around the overhead projector. Place one plastic transparency sheet on the overhead projector, and draw a straight pathway and a simple maze design on the transparency sheet with the permanent marker. Then sprinkle a few iron filings onto the sheet. Lay another plastic transparency sheet on top, and turn on the overhead projector light.

Say: **Watch! I can guide these iron filings through the maze.** Demonstrate how to do this, drawing the magnet through the maze along the top transparency sheet. Ask:

- **What is happening?**
- **Why are the iron filings moving?**

Say: **I am using a magnet to move the iron**

Scientist's Strategy

If you can't find iron filings in a store that sells educational supplies, most machine shops have a ready supply that they sweep off the floor every day! You won't need many for this activity. If time allows, let kids create their own paths on transparency sheets.

filings. Magnets attract or are attracted to other metals such as iron, steel, nickel, and cobalt. Magnetism is such a strong force that it can even work through some materials such as plastic.

Just like this maze zigs and zags, sometimes you may feel like your life doesn't have a very clear direction. Ask:

● **Can you think of a time it seemed like your life was zigging or zagging? Explain.**

Now move the iron filings to the straight path, and use the magnet to move them along in a straight line. Say: **Other times, you may feel like you're traveling on a straight path.** Ask:

● **Can you think of a time your life felt like a straight, easy path? Explain.**

Say: **Just as the magnet moved the iron filings down the maze and down the straight path, God is working in our lives no matter what. Whether you feel like your life is a maze or an easy path, you can know that God, like the magnet, will guide you always.**

Small Movers

EXPLORATION ELEMENT: Show kids the power of static electricity, and help them discover how important they are in God's eyes.

BIBLE BENCHMARKS: "Don't let anyone look down on you because you are young, but set an example for the believers in speech, in life, in love, in faith and in purity" (1 Timothy 4:12).

"A little child will lead them" (Isaiah 11:6b).

SUPPLIES: You'll need a Bible; a sink or a five-gallon jug of water with a spout, a stool, a large pan or bucket to catch the water, and plastic to put on the floor; a balloon for each child; a piece of wool or a carpet sample to charge the balloon; and a permanent marker.

ck • Light • Salt • Living Water • Amazing Science Devotions for Children's Ministry

PREPARATION: If you're going to use this devotion at children's time during a church service or if you don't have ready access to a sink, you'll need to set up your running water ahead of time. Lay plastic on the floor, and set the five-gallon jug of water on a stool. Put a large pan or bucket on the floor under the spigot to catch the water. When it's time for running water, just turn on the spigot.

Ask:

● **Whose opinion do you really value? Why?**

● **Who helps you understand the Bible?**

Say: **Hmm...most of these people are adults.** Ask:

● **Why doesn't another child teach you?**

● **What do you think would happen if next Sunday you decided to teach Sunday school?**

Scientist's Strategy

For maximum participation, let kids take turns holding the balloon and changing the course of water. Can they make the water stream "dance"?

Say: **Our experiment today is going to show you how important you are and how much you have to share.** Ask a volunteer to blow up the balloon and tie it off (or do this yourself if you're working with younger kids). Have another child rub the balloon on the wool fabric to charge it with static electricity. Make sure the child doesn't rub too hard! Turn on the faucet so it's running in a slow stream. Ask:

● **Do you think there's anything that can make this stream of water go in a different direction? Why?**

Slowly bring the balloon close to the water. Do not let the balloon touch the water because that will uncharge the balloon. As the balloon gets close to the water, the stream of water will curve out toward the balloon! Ask:

● **What happened? Why?**

● **What caused the water to move?**

Say: **Static electricity made the water move. When we rubbed the balloon on the carpet, it charged the balloon with electricity. The charge attracted the water to the balloon because water is a conductor of electricity. This means electricity can travel through water.** Ask:

click! Living Wat

● **Did you know that something as weak as static electricity could change the course of running water?**

Read aloud 1 Timothy 4:12, and ask:

● **What do you think this Scripture means?**

Say: **This Scripture says not to let anyone look down on you because you're young. You're important, and you can make a difference!** Ask:

● **What causes a child to be able to change something?**

● **Can you think of a time you made a difference in someone's life?**

Read aloud Isaiah 11:6a, and say: **Just as static electricity changed the course of running water, you can change someone else's life with God's help! You are very important in God's eyes, and he has big plans for you.**

Draw happy faces on balloons with a permanent marker, and give one to each child as a reminder that he or she is important.

Jesus, Our Circuit Connector

> **ExPLORATION ELEMENT:** Create a complete circuit of electricity as you show kids that Jesus is our connection to God.

BIBLE BENCHMARK: "Therefore he is able to save completely those who come to God through him, because he always lives to intercede for them" (Hebrews 7:25).

SUPPLIES: You'll need a Bible, a six-volt battery, a light, a switch, three pieces of wire, and a screwdriver. (These supplies can be purchased at a hardware store.)

PREPARATION: Be sure that the switch is off at the beginning of this devotion.

If time permits, have kids help you construct the circuit. One piece of wire should run from the battery to the light, the second one should run from the light to the switch, and the third wire should run from the switch to the battery as illustrated in the diagram. If you're short on time, come with the circuit already constructed.

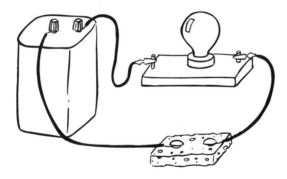

Say: **We have everything we need for the light to shine—a source** (point to the battery) **and wiring** (point to the wires) **that**

connects the source to the light. But the light isn't shining, so something must be wrong. Maybe we need to check the connections.** Have kids check each connection, and say: **The light still isn't shining.** Ask:

● **Does anyone know what could be wrong?**

Let kids discuss the problem. Hopefully, they'll realize that the switch needs to be on in order to make a complete circuit. If not, guide them to this understanding.

Say: **In order for the light to shine, the circuit—or pathway—has to be complete from the source to the light. The switch is off, so the power can't reach the light.** Have one child turn the switch on, and say: **Now we have a complete circuit, and the light shines. I have a Scripture to share with you.** Read aloud Hebrews 7:25. Ask:

● **Does anyone know what "intercede" means?**

Say: **A person who intercedes is someone who acts as a go-between, just as the switch—or the circuit connector—did in our experiment. The switch acted as a go-between for the wires and created a complete circuit.** Ask:

● **Does anyone in your life act as a circuit connector? Explain.**

● **What connects you to God?**

Say: **The Scripture says that Jesus intercedes for you. That means he talks to God for you; he is your go-between or circuit connector. Because of Jesus, you have a complete circuit with God.** Ask:

● **What are some things that can only shine out of your life when you're connected to God through Jesus?**

Push the switch down, turning on the light. Say: **Your life can shine with God's love because Jesus is in your life, completing your circuit to God! Awesome!**

Science Devotions for Children's Ministry

Let Your Light Shine

EXPLORATION ELEMENT: Have kids experiment with materials to find out which are conductors of electricity as they explore how they can be conductors of God's love.

BIBLE BENCHMARK: "In the same way, let your light shine before men, that they may see your good deeds and praise your Father in heaven" (Matthew 5:16).

SUPPLIES: You'll need a Bible; a six-volt battery; three pieces of wire; a light; two metal thumbtacks; cork or cardboard; and a variety of materials to test, such as coins, buttons, pencils, erasers, keys, glass, and balloons.

PREPARATION: None is needed.

If time permits, have kids help you construct the circuit. Stick the thumbtacks in the cork, and run one piece of wire from the battery to the light. Run the second piece of wire from the light to one thumbtack, and run the third piece of wire from the battery to the other thumbtack. If you're short on time, come with the circuit already constructed.

Ask:

● **Does anyone know what a conductor is?**

Say: **Let's do an experiment to discover what a conductor is.** Bring out your circuit so kids can see it. Ask:

● **Why doesn't this light shine?**

Say: **This circuit has a battery, and all the wires are connected.** Have kids check the connections to be sure they are hooked up properly.

Point out that the circuit is not complete between the two tacks. Say: **We don't have a complete connection. We need to add something here to make a complete circuit—something the electricity can flow through. Let's try some things I have here to see what will work.** Let kids take turns trying various items, laying them on both of the tacks to complete the circuit. Ask:

● What do you notice about these materials?

● Why do some of the materials work and others don't?

Scientist's Strategy

For maximum partici-
pation, have kids cre-
ate their own circuits
and experiment with
conductors in groups
of three or four.

Say: **Some of the materials conduct electricity. That means that electricity can flow through them. Others do not conduct electricity.**

Read aloud Matthew 5:16, and say: **Did you know you can be a conductor of God's love? Some things make you a good conductor, ready to be used by God.** Ask:

● **What are some of these things?**

● **How can you know how to be a good conductor of God's love?**

● **Is there anything you can do to learn what God wants?**

Say: **One way you can learn to be a good conductor of God's love is by reading and studying his Word. This helps you learn more about what God is like so you can tell other people.**

Say: **When you let God's love flow through you, you're being a good conductor. Your light is shining just as the electric light shines when it has a good conductor to make a complete circuit. When you live your life as God wants you to, your light shines and people can see God through you.**

The Battle of the Balloons

BIBLE BENCHMARK: "Enter through the narrow gate. For wide is the gate and broad is the road that leads to destruction, and many enter through it. But small is the gate and narrow the road that leads to life, and only a few find it" (Matthew 7:13-14).

SUPPLIES: You'll need a Bible, two nine-inch balloons, two twist ties, and an empty thread spool.

PREPARATION: None is needed.

Ask:

● **Do you think it's easy or difficult to follow God? Explain.**

Say: **Today we're going to do an experiment that will remind us of where God wants us to be.**

Have a child blow up one balloon almost to capacity—about the size of a soccer ball—and tie off the balloon with a twist tie. Have a second child partially blow up the second balloon; it should be a little bigger than a grapefruit. Tie off the second balloon with a twist tie, too. Keep the balloons tied, and stretch the end of each balloon over an end of the spool. Take the twist tie off the small balloon. Ask:

● **What do you think will happen if I take the twist tie off the large balloon? Why?**

Ask one of the kids to untie the second balloon. The air from the small balloon will move into the large balloon. Ask:

● **What happened?**

Scientist's Strategy

If you have a time limit for this devotion, you can blow up the balloons and mount them on the spool ahead of time.

Power ● Heavens ● Earth ● Wind ● Bread ● Storm ● Garden ● Compass ● Rainbow ● Creati

● **Did you expect the big balloon to get bigger?**

● **Why do you think this happened?**

Say: **The air molecules in the small balloon are more crowded than the air molecules in the big balloon. This makes the pressure greater in the small balloon. When the balloons are untied, the pressure in the small balloon pushes the air molecules into the large balloon.**

Read aloud Matthew 7:13-14, and ask:

● **Can anyone see a relationship between these verses and what happened to the balloons? Explain.**

● **Which balloon represents the wide road?**

● **How is life on the wide road?**

Say: **The wide road in life is the easy way. When you live your life on the wide road, it means you do what everyone else is doing even if it isn't right.** Ask:

● **Which balloon represents the narrow road?**

● **How is life on the narrow road?**

Say: **The narrow road is the right way, but sometimes it's hard to stay there. Your friends might make fun of you for doing the right thing and staying on the narrow road.** Ask:

● **Has this ever happened to you? Explain.**

● **What can you do when this happens to you?**

Say: **When people make fun of you for doing the right thing, you need to be very careful. It's so easy to let wrong**

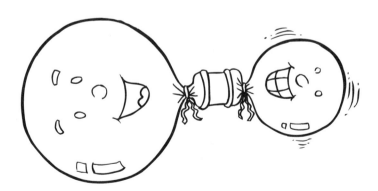

ideas influence you. When this happens, you can get pulled onto the wide road and away from the right way, much in the same way that all the air got sucked out of the small balloon and into the larger balloon. God wants you to follow his way even though it's not always easy. But God will help you and give you the strength to stay on the narrow road.

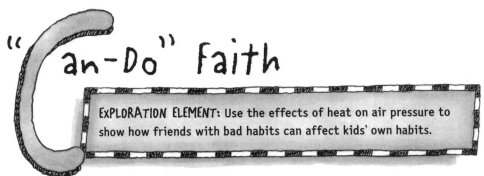

"Can-Do" Faith

ExPLORATION ELEMENT: Use the effects of heat on air pressure to show how friends with bad habits can affect kids' own habits.

BIBLE BENCHMARK: "Do not be misled: 'Bad company corrupts good character' " (1 Corinthians 15:33).

SUPPLIES: You'll need a Bible, a saucepan, an empty aluminum soda can, a measuring spoon, water, tongs, newspaper, and a cookie sheet.

OPTIONAL SUPPLIES: You may want a portable electric deep-fryer.

PREPARATION: It would be best to do this devotion in the church kitchen so you could use a stovetop, but use an electric deep-fryer if you can't use the church kitchen. Before class, bring about an inch of water to a boil in either the saucepan or the deep-fryer so it's boiling when kids arrive. Spread newspaper near the saucepan, place the cookie sheet near the saucepan, and fill the cookie sheet with cold water.

Gather kids around the saucepan, and say: **Let's pretend that you and I are like this can. The smooth sides of this can represent how we look when we have habits that make God happy.** Ask:
• **What kinds of habits make God happy?**

Read aloud 1 Corinthians 15:33, and say: **We can do an experiment that will help us get a picture of what this verse means.** Measure

and pour one teaspoon of water into the empty soda can, and place the can upright in the saucepan. The water will need to boil for several minutes until the can is filled with steam. When the water has boiled for several minutes, ask:

Stress to kids that to keep from being burned, they need to avoid touching the stovetop, the saucepan, or the soda can.

- **What do you notice about the water in the pan?**

- **What do you think has happened to the water inside the can?**

Say: **Air pressure is an invisible power. Did you know that air presses down on things? Normally when the air pushes on an object, that object pushes back with the same strength. The heat inside the can is making the air expand, or take up more space. There is only so much space inside the can, so some air is being forced out of the can in the form of steam. Let's pretend that the air pressure outside the can represents bad influences.** Ask:

- **What things make some people the wrong kind of friends to have?**

- **What do you think will happen to your good habits if you spend too much time with friends with bad habits?**

Say: **Let's see the effects of air pressure on this can.**

Use tongs to remove the can from the saucepan, and immediately flip the can with its top downward into the cookie sheet of cold water. Turn off the stove, and ask:

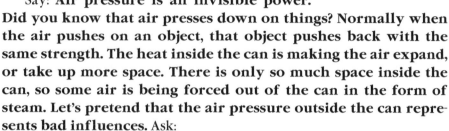

- **Now that the can isn't in boiling water, do you think the air inside the can is going to get warmer or cooler? Explain.**

Say: **Cooler air takes up less space. The scientific word for taking up less space is "contracting."** Ask:

Try this experiment ahead of time to determine how long it will take to boil the water. You don't want to be left with "dead time" while you're waiting for the water to boil. It may help to start with hot tap water.

- **If less air is in the can, do you think it will have more or less air pressure? Why?**

Have kids watch the can to see what happens. When the can is crushed, ask:

- **Why do you think the can collapsed?**

wer ∗ Heavens ∗ Earth ∗ Wind ∗ Bread ∗ Storm ∗ Garden ∗ Compass ∗ Rainbow ∗ Creation

• Do you think the air inside the can or the air outside the can had more pressure?

Say: **The steam pushed some air out of the can and lowered the pressure inside the can. The air pressure outside the can was more powerful than the pressure inside the can. Both the air inside and outside the can pushed on the can. The air pressure on the outside was stronger, and it changed the shape of the can. Even though we may not notice air or even know it has power, it can change the shape of things.** Ask:

• **How is the crumpled can like a person with the wrong friends?**

Say: **God told us to pick good friends and stay away from bad friends to protect the "shape" of our habits. All God's rules keep us safe and let us grow good habits that make him happy.**

Invisible but Real

EXPLORATION ELEMENT: Show kids how air creates an invisible barrier as you discuss the Holy Spirit at work in their lives.

BIBLE BENCHMARKS: "Don't you know that you yourselves are God's temple and that God's Spirit lives in you?" (1 Corinthians 3:16).

"Now faith is being sure of what we hope for and certain of what we do not see" (Hebrews 11:1).

SUPPLIES: You'll need a Bible, newspaper, a deep tub full of water, a clear drinking glass, and a paper towel.

PREPARATION: Spread the newspaper on a table or the floor, and set the tub of water, the drinking glass, and the paper towel on top of it.

Power ∗ Heavens ∗ Earth ∗ Wind ∗ Bread ∗ Storm ∗ Gar   ∗ Creati

Read aloud 1 Corinthians 3:16 and Hebrews 11:1, and say: **Let's do an experiment to help us understand that even though we can't see God's Spirit in us, he is still very real.**

Have kids gather around the newspaper, and have one child wad up the paper towel and put it in the bottom of the glass. Ask:

● **What do you think will happen to the paper towel if I put the glass in the tub of water?**

Turn the glass upside down and push it *straight* down into the tub of water. Make sure you get the glass completely under the water. Hold the glass underwater for a few seconds, and then carefully pull the glass straight up out of the water. Have a volunteer pull the paper towel out of the glass, and ask:

● **What do you notice about the paper towel?**

● **How can it still be dry?**

Say: **The glass looked empty, but it was actually full of air. When I pushed the glass into the water, an invisible wall of air was pushed back against the paper towel. This wall of air kept the paper towel from getting wet. We can't see the air, but it's still there. We saw evidence of it because the paper towel stayed dry.** Ask:

● **What gives you evidence that God is there even though you can't see him?**

Read aloud 1 Corinthians 3:16 again, or have a child read it for you. Say: **This Scripture says that the Holy Spirit lives in you.** Ask:

● **You can't see the Spirit, so how do you know the Spirit is in your life?**

Say: **Other people can see evidence of the Holy Spirit in your life in the way you treat them.** Ask:

● **Do you think you treat other people the way Jesus wants you to? Explain.**

Read aloud Hebrews 11:1 again, or have a child read it for you. Ask:

● **What helps us to know that something**

Scientist's Strategy

If you're doing this devotion during a time other than children's time in church, perhaps you could have kids gather around a big sink to do the experiment. For maximum participation, let kids take turns trying it. Experiment with what happens if you let a little air escape as you push the glass down and what happens if you let a little air escape on the way back up.

is there when we're not able to see it?

Say: **By faith, we know that God's Spirit is in us. This verse from Hebrews tells us we can be sure of what we don't see. We can't see the Spirit, but we can be sure he's there, in us, helping us to live like Jesus wants us to. Just as the air kept the paper towel dry, the Spirit helps us.**

All Scripture Is Given by God

EXPLORATION ELEMENT: Use the effects of a vacuum to help kids discover that they can trust what the Bible says because it came from the Holy Spirit through faithful people.

BIBLE BENCHMARK: "All Scripture is God-breathed" (2 Timothy 3:16a).

SUPPLIES: You'll need a Bible, newspaper, a drinking glass full of water, a drinking straw, scissors, a paper towel, and food coloring.

OPTIONAL SUPPLIES: You may want extra straws and glasses.

PREPARATION: Spread newspaper on a table or the floor, and set the glass of water on it. Squirt a few drops of food coloring into the water.

Have kids gather around the newspaper, and read aloud 2 Timothy 3:16a. Ask:

● **What do you think this verse means?**

Say: **This verse tells us that everything in the Bible is given to us directly from God. Let's see how this might work.**

Cut a horizontal slit about one-third of the distance from one end of the straw. Bend the straw at the slit, and hold the short section in the glass of water. Be sure to keep the slit about one-fourth inch above the surface of the water.

Say: **The colored water is like all the words the Bible writers knew how to say. But remember, the only words in the Bible are words that were given by God.**

Hold the paper towel up behind the slit, and ask for a volunteer to blow into the long side of the straw. Ask:

● **What's happening to the paper towel?**

Try tilting the straw a little, and have your volunteer keep blowing until water moves up the straw and colors the paper towel. Ask:

● **How does this experiment get water from the glass to blow onto the paper towel?**

Say: **When you blow across the slit, it pulls the air out of the bottom part of the straw. This produces a vacuum, or a space that has absolutely nothing in it. To fill the vacuum, water from the glass is drawn up the straw and then blown onto the paper towel.**

Ask:

- Could the colored water have gotten onto the paper towel if you hadn't blown on it?

- How is this like God using people to write the Bible?

- Could people have written the Bible without the Holy Spirit's help? Why or why not?

Say: **We know that the words in the Bible are God's words even though they were written down by people just like you and me. Through the Holy Spirit, God worked within the hearts and minds of the Bible writers to help them write down his truth. We can trust that the things God tells us in the Bible are right.**

Scientist's Strategy

For maximum participation, provide several straws and glasses of colored water to allow more kids to try the experiment.

Reflecting God

EXPLORATION ELEMENT: Have kids view their reflections in various items, and compare the experience to ways we can reflect God in the world.

BIBLE BENCHMARK: "Now we see but a poor reflection as in a mirror; then we shall see face to face. Now I know in part; then I shall know fully, even as I am fully known" (1 Corinthians 13:12).

SUPPLIES: You'll need a Bible, several small mirrors, aluminum foil, and several large metal spoons.

PREPARATION: None is needed.

Power * Heavens * Earth * Wind * Bread * Storm * Garden * Compass * Rainbow * Creatio

84

Ask:

- **How can you find out what you look like?**

Say: **Today we're going to be looking into some different items to discover what we look like.** Have kids form groups of two to four, and give each group a small mirror, a piece of aluminum foil, and a large metal spoon. Say: **I've given you several items that will reflect how you look. Take a few moments to discover the differences in your reflections in the different items.** After a few moments, ask:

- **Which item gave you the most distorted reflection?**
- **In which item did you see a very dull reflection?**
- **Which item gave you the clearest reflection?**

Say: **Now I'd like you to think about the way your life might reflect God.** Ask:

- **Which way do you think God would want to be reflected?**
- **How do you feel you reflect God?**

Read aloud 1 Corinthians 13:12, and say: **A reflection of God was given to us when Jesus came to earth. He loved the unlovable, he spent time with people others considered unworthy, and he cared for people who needed comfort.**

God truly needs us to be reflections of him. God has called us to continue this reflection in order to share him with the world.

Think about how your reflection looked in the spoon. It was distorted, wasn't it? God doesn't want you to be a distorted reflection of him to the world. Ask:

- **How could you be a distorted reflection of God?**

Say: **Think about the way your reflection looked in the aluminum foil. It was kind of dull. God doesn't want you to be a dull reflection of him in the world, either.** Ask:

- **How could you be a dull reflection of God?**

Say: **Now think about the way your reflection looked in the mirror.** Ask:

- **How could you be a clear reflection of God?**

ock • Light   Amazing Science Devotions for Children's Ministry

More Than Meets the Eye

EXPLORATION ELEMENT: Use the colorful concepts of chromatography and adhesion to help kids understand that God sees what's in our hearts.

BIBLE BENCHMARK: "The Lord does not look at the things man looks at. Man looks at the outward appearance, but the Lord looks at the heart" (1 Samuel 16:7b).

SUPPLIES: You'll need a Bible, newspaper, cone-shaped coffee filters, small clear plastic cups, a pitcher of water, and black felt-tip pens with water-soluble ink.

PREPARATION: Spread newspaper on a table or on the floor.

Have kids gather around the newspaper. Read aloud 1 Samuel 16:7b, and say: **Let's try to understand this verse more clearly.** Hold up a felt-tip pen, and ask:

- **What color is this pen? Are you sure?**
- **Does everyone agree that the pen is black?**

Give each child a coffee filter, a plastic cup, and a felt-tip pen. Pour about half an inch of water in each child's cup. Say: **This water can remind us of the effect God's love has on our lives because God's love is as deep and wide as all the water in an ocean.** Have each child draw a stick figure about one inch tall near the bottom edge of the large side of his or her coffee filter.

Have kids place their filters in their cups with the tips of the cones pointing up. Say: **Let's pretend that putting our stick figures into the water is like God looking at us to see what we're like.**

Wait until the colors begin to separate. Ask:

- **What is happening to your stick figure?**
- **What direction on the coffee filter is the water moving?**

Power • Heavens • Earth • Wind • Bread • Storm • Garden • Compass • Rainbow • Creatio

Say: **The scientific word for the water climbing up the coffee filter is "adhesion." This means that the water is being pulled up the filter when normally gravity would make the water fall down.** Ask:

● **What do you notice about your black stick figure?**

● **How many different colors do you see?**

Say: **The scientific word used to describe how colors separate is "chromatography." Sometimes what looks like one color is really many colors combined together.**

● **What does this tell you about what God sees when he looks at you?**

Say: **When you try to get to know someone, you can see only what's on the outside. It's like what you saw when you looked at your stick figure; all you could see was a single color. But because God loves you so much, he has the ability to look inside your heart and see everything inside you.** Ask:

● **What things do you think God can see inside you?**

● **What kinds of things do you think God likes to see inside you?**

● **What kinds of things does God not like to see inside you?**

Scientist's Strategy

If you don't have black felt-tip pens, test other colors before you do the experiment. Some dark colored pens may work, but lighter colored pens won't work. If you have extra time, you might want to let kids experiment with different colored pens or markers to see which ones will work and what colors they produce.

Say: **God can see what's in our hearts all the time. Sometimes what he sees makes him happy, and other times it makes him sad. God loves us very much, and he wants to see good things when he looks into our hearts.**

Rainbow Promises

EXPLORATION ELEMENT: Show kids how rainbows are created as you remind them of God's promises to them.

BIBLE BENCHMARK: "I have set my rainbow in the clouds, and it will be the sign of the covenant between me and the earth. Whenever I bring clouds over the earth and the rainbow appears in the clouds, I will remember my covenant between me and you and all living creatures of every kind" (Genesis 9:13-15a).

SUPPLIES: You'll need a Bible, a drinking glass full of water, a large index card, scissors, transparent tape, white paper, and newsprint and a marker or a chalkboard and chalk.

PREPARATION: Cut a one-half-inch vertical slit in the center of the index card.

Tell the story of Noah and the ark or read the account found in Genesis before beginning this activity. Then read aloud Genesis 9:13-15a.

Say: **After the great flood, God promised Noah that there would never be another flood that destroyed the earth. The token of God's promise was a rainbow in the sky, which God said would remind him of his promise to all the living creatures of the earth.**

It is awesome to look at the sky after a storm and see a rainbow among the disappearing clouds. When we see a rainbow, we can remember that it stands for a promise from God to all of us.

To help us remember God's promise, let's make our own rainbows!

Scientist's Strategy
You'll need a sunny day for this devotion. The sunlight's intensity makes a difference, so try to do the experiment as close to the brightest part of the day as you can.

Tape the index card with the vertical slit cut in it to one side of the glass.

Set a piece of white paper on a flat surface near a window, and place the glass of water on it so the sun shines through the slit in the index card first, then through the water in the glass and onto the white paper (see illustration).

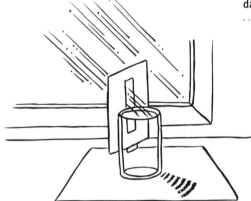

A spectrum of colors should appear on the white paper. You may have to adjust the glass a bit to get the best color spread. Ask:

● **What caused the sun shining through the glass to form a rainbow?**

Say: **When the light shone through the glass, it was refracted, or bent, by the water in the glass. When light rays are refracted, it causes them to separate into their separate color components. In the same way, the moisture in the air after a storm causes sunlight to be refracted into rainbows in the atmosphere.**

You may have noticed that the spectrum of colors that makes up rainbows is always in the same order. Have kids call out the colors in the spectrum, starting with red. Ask:

● **Why do you think the colors are always in the same order?**

Say: **This happens because different colors of light rays have different wavelengths. Colors with long wavelengths, such as red, bend more than colors with shorter wavelengths, such as** violet. The colors in the spectrum fan out in a curve, and voilà! It's a rainbow!

There's an easy way to remember the order of the colors in a rainbow; some of you may already know it. It sounds just like a person's name. It's **Roy G. Biv.** Write this on a piece of newsprint, and show kids how each letter in the name stands for one color in the spectrum (red, orange, yellow, green, blue, indigo, and violet). Have kids call out God's promises or character traits that start with each of the letters in Roy G. Biv.

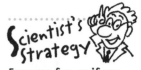

For more fun, or if you have extra time, have kids stand in a place that allows you to aim the "rainbow" at them. Have them chant the spectrum colors in order every time someone "wears" the rainbow!

Say: **God uses rainbows to remind himself of the promise he made to us.** Ask:

- **How do you remember promises you make to others?**
- **Have you ever forgotten a promise you made?**
- **Has God ever forgotten his promise to you?**
- **How important is it to keep a promise?**
- **How would you feel if someone broke a promise to you?**
- **How do you think someone would feel if you broke a promise to him or her?**
- **Since God still honors the promise he made to us and rainbows still appear after storms, how important do you think it is to honor your promises to God?**
- **What kinds of promises can you make to God?**

Say: **The next time you see a rainbow, remember God's promises to you, and remember how important it is to keep your promises to God.**

Indexes

Scripture Index

Power * Heavens * Earth * Wind * Bread * Storm * Garden * Compass * Rainbow * Creat

Subject Index

ock • Light • Salt • Living Water • Amazing Science Devotions for Children's Ministry

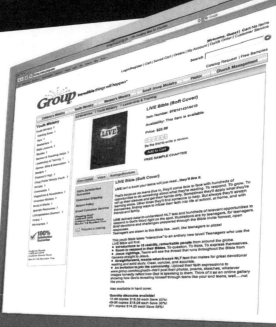